ADVENTURES IN TIME

STUDIES IN PSYCHICAL RESEARCH

Series editor: Dr John Beloff, University of Edinburgh

Tony Cornell *Investigating the Paranormal: Spontaneous Cases and Other Related Phenomena.*

Adventures in Time

Encounters with the Past

ANDREW MACKENZIE

THE ATHLONE PRESS
London & Atlantic Highlands, NJ

First published 1997 by
THE ATHLONE PRESS LTD
1 Park Drive, London NW11 7SG
and 165 First Avenue,
Atlantic Highlands, NJ 07716

British Library Cataloguing in Publication Data
*A catalogue record for this book is available
from the British Library*

ISBN 0 485 82001 3

Library of Congress Cataloging-in-Publication Data

MacKenzie, Andrew.
    Adventures in time : encounters with the past / Andrew
MacKenzie ; with an introduction by Alan Gauld.
        p.   cm. -- (Studies in psychic research)
    Includes bibliographical references and index.
    ISBN 0-485-82001-3 (hardcover)
    1. Retrocognition.   I. Title.   II. Series.
BF1339.M33   1997
133.8--dc21
                                                        97-480
                                                        CIP

Typeset by Bibloset in 10pt Plantin

Printed and bound in Great Britain by
Bookcraft (Bath) Ltd

Contents

The world is not only queerer than anyone has imagined but queerer than anyone can imagine.

(J. B. S. Haldane)

The world is a very odd place and there are very odd people and events in it.

(C. D. Broad)

There really are more things in the world than the science of any period can fully account for.

(Gilbert Murray)

There may be some things that the human intellect will never understand and some phenomena that will never be explained.

(John Beloff)

It is my opinion that our present picture of physical reality, particularly in relation to the nature of *time*, is due for a grand shake-up – even greater, perhaps, than that which has already been provided by present-day relativity and quantum mechanics.

(Roger Penrose)

The hope that new experiments will lead us back to objective events in time and space is about as well founded as the hope of discovering the end of the world in the unexplored regions of the Antarctic.

(Werner Heisenberg)

We know very little about the universe, and it may well be a much queerer place than most of us think.

(H. H. Price)

Acknowledgements

I wish to thank the editor of the *Journal* and *Proceedings* of the Society for Psychical Research (the SPR) for permission to quote from the society's publications. In the investigation of the Kersey case I wish to thank particularly Dr Hugh Pincott, a former Hon. Secretary of the SPR, for his help in the field, Mr A. E. B. Owen, Keeper of Manuscripts in the library of the University of Cambridge, for his help in searching medieval documents relating to the village, and in the village itself Mr Leslie Cockayne for his advice with the interpretation of local history, particularly that relating to Bridge House, and Mrs Jillian Finch, the present owner of Bridge House. The Rev. Gerald Harrison, a former rector of Kersey, kindly helped me by referring me to residents of the village who had knowledge of the past. Officials of the Suffolk Record Office at Ipswich and Bury St Edmunds were most helpful, as were staff of the area surveyor's office in the Highways Department of the Suffolk County Council at Bury St Edmunds. I am most grateful to the principal witness in the Kersey case, Mr William Laing, of Leuras, New South Wales, for bringing the case to my attention and for his great patience in answering the many questions I addressed to him. It was his steadfastness in sticking to his story that convinced me more than anything else that the case, one of great rarity, was genuine, supported, as it was, by evidence. I wish to thank Macdonald & Watson, Little Ltd, licensing agents, for permission to quote Jane Forman's *The Mask of Time* (1978), J. M. Dent & Sons for permission to quote from Paul Davies's *God and the New Physics* (1983), Bantam Press for permission to quote from Stephen Hawking's *A Brief History of Time* (1988) and Oxford University Press for permission to quote from Roger Penrose's *The Emperor's New Mind* (1989).

Introduction

Psychical research, or parapsychology as it has increasingly come to be called under American auspices, suffers from the unique misfortune that many of those who write in its support do it more harm than its most vociferous critics. The prejudices and over-simplifications of its critics are often blatantly obvious and are likely to command the assent only of those antecedently disposed to the same viewpoint. But if anything could make one lean towards the critics it is the excesses of many supporters. Go into any large bookshop and you will find under the heading 'Parapsychology' numerous books on precognition, predictions, apparitions, hauntings, poltergeists, telepathy, mediums, even astrology and visitors from outer space, the majority of which are filled with stories that, as narrated, have almost no claims to credibility. The authors either do not know that proper evidence is and how to present it, or else are deliberately writing for a wholly gullible readership. Any reasonably intelligent person who picked over this literature with the idea that there might be matters here worth investigating would soon give up.

To those who, like myself, feel after studying in some detail the first-hand evidence for phenomena of some of the kinds in question, and after personally investigating a number of cases, that when every allowance is made for common sources of error there remains a residuum of curious phenomena worthy of serious attention, all this is highly regrettable. Fortunately there are just a few writers whose works significantly redress the balance. One of them is Mr Andrew MacKenzie who over the last quarter of a century has produced a series of books on what might be called the 'spontaneous' (as opposed to the 'laboratory') phenomena of psychical research. That is to say, he has written about phenomena that have come, or largely come, unsought, out of the blue. These have included cases of fulfilled premonitions, poltergeists not readily ascribable to trickery, apparitions of the dead and the dying, and hauntings (in which the same apparition is seen by different witnesses independently of each other). Although Mr MacKenzie addresses himself to the general reader, he never loses sight of the canons of evidence requisite in this field. He deals in the first-hand signed statements of eye-witnesses; he obtains whatever documentary support is appropriate; he is well aware of the need to guard against the various possible sources of error in testimony. And he is not (as are so many writers on these topics) content merely to retell and re-examine cases already in print. He has been an extensive case-collector in his own right and has perhaps as wide an experience of the problems of case investigation as anyone in the country.

In this his latest volume, Mr MacKenzie presents cases of apparent retrocognition; cases, that is, of ostensible direct awareness, not ordinarily explicable, of past scenes and events. Such cases are fascinating, exceedingly rare and very hard to evaluate. In addition to the usual problems of witness reliability, mistakes of memory, intrusion of the imagination, and so forth, verification of the details of the witness's statement is likely to be especially difficult, and of course the more distant in time the scene or events ostensibly retrocognized, the greater will the difficulty become. Sometimes, too, one has seriously to consider the possibility that the witness may have mistaken some actual contemporary scene or event for a retrocognitive vision of the past. This is a particular danger in cases in which the witness did not at the time think his or her experience abnormal or paranormal but only came to suppose it so on later reflection. All these pitfalls are fully and fairly examined by Mr MacKenzie, and the fact that he none the less regards certain cases as constituting evidence for retrocognition is correspondingly noteworthy.

As well as reviewing and analysing classic cases, and some less well-known ones, Mr MacKenzie presents several cases which he has investigated himself. One of these, which forms the subject of Chapter 1, is among the most curious and detailed so far published and constitutes a significant addition to the literature. It is destined to become a classic of the genre.

Anyone who reads this book is bound to ask himself or herself what precognition and retrocognition, if they indeed occur, tell us about the universe we live in and our relation to it. In his final chapter Mr MacKenzie indicates various lines of speculation and notes some recurrent characteristics of the retrocognitive experiences themselves. But, as he would be the first to agree, we can only speculate; interesting though the speculations are, firm knowledge eludes us. Our prime need is for more data. In recommending *Adventures in Time* to a wide readership, I would particularly draw attention to its last paragraph. Those who can offer further case material are urged to communicate with Mr MacKenzie at the address given.

Department of Psychology   *Alan Gauld*
University of Nottingham

Preface

This is, I believe, the first book to be devoted solely to retrocognition, defined in the *Oxford English Dictionary* as 'knowledge of the past supernaturally acquired', the most controversial, most puzzling and rarest of all psychical phenomena. It deals with the seemingly impossible, the experiencing of the past in the present, whether in visionary form or, in very rare cases, being able to walk through an area and see it as it was in the past with features of the present day obliterated. Those involved in such an experience are hallucinated, which may be explained as being in an altered state of consciousness. Some hallucinatory experiences, particularly those induced by drink or drugs, or resulting from mental illness, are bizarre in the extreme, but others, occurring to sane people in good health, convey information that can be checked and are known as veridical. For nearly a century the best-known case of ostensible retrocognition has been the famous 'adventure' of Miss Moberly and Miss Jourdain, two English academics, in the park of the Petit Trianon at Versailles in 1901, an account of which, under the title of *An Adventure* was published ten years later and ran through many editions, arousing enormous interest that continues until the present.

However, no other case of similar importance came to light, and *An Adventure* might have remained as a solitary curiosity had not a case containing many similar features to the Versailles 'adventure' reached me from a reader in Australia, Mr William Laing, whose letter of 20 July 1988 described how, while a boy undergoing training at a naval shore establishment in Suffolk in 1957, he and two companions walked into a small village, Kersey, and found it as it could have been after the Black Death in 1349, silent and deserted.

This, if it could be confirmed, seemed too good to be true, for I had been waiting for thirty years for such a case to come my way, but Mr Laing, an ex-Royal Navy wireless operator, gave the name of another witness, also in Australia, who could vouch for the truth of the account, which he in due course did. After a great deal of trouble, and many fruitless inquiries, the third member of the party was traced. He remembered being in the village with the others but that was all. This was disappointing, but perhaps, after a lapse of thirty years, the loss of memory was to be expected. However, I had the evidence of two witnesses who had a very vivid recollection of what had taken place in Kersey and I was able to start my research to see if what they had told me could be verified. In this I succeeded beyond my wildest expectations. The task of the psychical researcher is, as a rule, beset by disappointments as case after case collapses for lack of supporting evidence, or because of dubious evidence, but here at last was a case that stood up to close examination. The Kersey case, given here for the first time, is only the second of its type to come to light in a century and then only because an exceptionally good witness, Mr Laing, was willing to answer all my questions in what could be regarded as a severe grilling, which he took in good part as he wanted, as much as I did, to establish the truth.

Eventually, when Mr Laing came to England on holiday, we visited Kersey together and were able to check how the Kersey of 1990 differed from the Kersey he and his companions saw in 1957. There were vital differences. One side of the lane by which they entered the village from the southern end in 1957 had contained only forest trees but now was lined with cottages, the oldest of which were built in the fifteenth century. Where there had been no pubs north of the stream that runs through the village, there were now two of considerable age with signs prominently displayed, and, strangest of all, although while the youths had been in the village they had seen no church, now on a mound at the southern end of Kersey was a church whose large tower had been in place for more than five hundred years, and whose nave was considerably older than this.

The only commercial building seen by the three youths in the village was a butcher's shop with decaying meat in it. When I sent Mr Laing a postcard of the village as it is today he returned the card from Australia with an arrow indicating a building by the stream in the 'possible position' of the butcher's shop. Inquiries at the house concerned revealed that a butchery business had once been conducted from there. I was surprised to receive this confirmation.

A feature of both the Versailles case and the Kersey case was the strange silence noticed by the witnesses, an indication that they were in a trancelike state. An excellent description of the formation of such a state of mind is given by Miss Jourdain in an appendix in the fourth edition of *An Adventure* (1931). Describing a visit to the Petit Trianon on 12 September 1908 to take photographs she said:

> As the quickest way out of the grounds I went towards the old *logement du corps des gardes*, and as I turned the corner of the old wall I saw two women sitting in the shade, not far from the old gateway, which, in 1901, had been open and showed a well-kept drive within. They were disputing in loud voices. As I passed the *logement*, suddenly and utterly unexpectedly, I felt that some indefinable change had taken place. I felt as though I were being taken up into another condition of things quite as real as the former. The women's voices, though their quarrel was just as shrill and eager as before, seemed to be fading so quickly away that they would soon be gone altogether; from their tones the dispute was still clearly going on, but seemed to have less and less power to reach me.
>
> I turned to look back and saw the gates near which they were sitting melting away, and the background of trees again becoming visible through them, as on our original visit, but I noticed that the side pillars were standing steady (these pillars were old and probably had not been renewed since their original erection). The whole scene – sky, trees and buildings – gave a little shiver, like the movement of a curtain or of scenery as at a theatre.

(1931: 107)

We have here an example of a dispute still taking place being silenced as the witness felt herself being taken up 'into another condition of things quite as real as the former'. There can be variations on such an experience. One, quoted by the late Professor Gardner Murphy, an influential American psychologist, concerned a woman who, when carrying papers to a professor in Nebraska Wesleyan University, Lincoln, Nebraska, on 3 October 1963, entered a room and saw the figure of a very tall woman, with dark hair, reaching up to the shelves of a cabinet and standing perfectly still. In her account the woman who was carrying papers said, 'It was then that I was aware that there were no noises out in the hall. Everything was deathly quiet . . . she wasn't at all aware of my presence. While I was watching her, she never moved. She was not transparent and yet I knew she wasn't real. While I was looking at her, she just faded away – not parts of her body one at a time, but her whole body all at once.' It was later established that the description fitted that of a music teacher who had worked at the college from 1912 until her death in 1936. It will be noted that during the experience 'everything was deathly quiet', a characteristic of many of the experiences of this type.

Sceptics may argue that all such accounts are suspect, and that those that are to follow in this book are suspect because we know little about the powers of observation of the people concerned or, indeed, about their mental stability at the time. In opposition to this view one may quote the experience of a trained observer, the famous astronomer Sir John Herschel, FRS, who did much to extend the powers of the telescope, as set out in his *Familiar Lectures on Scientific Subjects*:

> I had been witnessing the demolition of a structure familiar to me from childhood and with which many interesting associations were connected; a demolition not unattended with danger to the workmen, about which I had felt very uncomfortable. It happened to me at the approach of evening, while, however, there was yet good light to pass under the place where the day before it had stood; the path I had to follow leading beside it. Great was my amazement to see it as if standing – projected against the dull sky. Being perfectly aware that it was a mere nervous impression, I walked on keeping my eyes directed to it, and the perspective and disposition of the parts appeared to change with the change in the point of view as they could have done if real. I ought to add that nothing of the kind had ever occurred to me before or has occurred since.
>
> (1867: 405)

There can be no question here of Sir John mistaking a building that he thought had been demolished for one still standing; he had been familiar with it since childhood and passed close to it. It is a pity he did not record how long the experience lasted. What he called 'a mere nervous impression' is what we today would call an hallucination. Many doctors refuse to regard hallucinations as anything other than the products of disturbed minds and often ascribe such experiences to schizophrenia. The difficulty we face here, I feel, is to find a word, or term, to describe what happens during experiences of the kind recorded in this book.

Phrases such as 'being caught in a time warp', or a 'time slip', are commonly used to describe experiences involving retrocognition, but they explain nothing. Instead we should turn to the nature of hallucinations and the mysteries associated with time. An hallucination is defined in the *Oxford Pocket Dictionary* as 'Illusion; apparent perception of object not present', but this definition is far from satisfactory. An hallucination is much more than an illusion and the perception can be much more than 'apparent'. The great American psychologist William James said in his *Principles of Psychology* (1890) that hallucinations are often talked of as *mental images* projected outwards by mistake. 'But when an hallucination is complete, it is much more than a mental image. An hallucination is a strictly sensational form of consciousness, as good and true a sensation as if there were a real object there. The object happens not to be there, that is all.'

Most of us live with a conception of time that involves past, present and future. The past has irretrievably gone, the present is now and the future has yet to be experienced, or so we think. But is this really so? Let us consider what some scientists have to say about this. Dr Stephen W. Hawking, Lucasian Professor of Mathematics at Cambridge University, points out in his highly acclaimed book *A Brief History of Time* that both Aristotle and Newton believed in absolute time and that time was completely separate from and independent of space. This is what most people would take to be the common-sense view. However, we have had to change our ideas about space and time. Although our apparently common-sense notions work well when dealing with things like apples, or with planets that travel comparatively slowly, they do not work at all for things moving at or near the speed of light. The theory of relativity forces us to change fundamentally our ideas of space and time. We must accept that time is not completely separate from and independent of space, but is combined with it to form an object called space-time. There was no unique absolute time. The laws of science did not distinguish between the forward and backward directions of time.

Professor Hawking concedes the theoretical possibility of travel
into the past. Discussing back holes, a region of space-time from
which nothing, not even light, can escape because gravity is so
strong, he considers the plight of an astronaut who fell into a
black hole:

> There are some solutions of the equations of general relativity in
> which it is possible for our astronaut to see a naked singularity (a
> point in space-time at which the space-time curvature becomes
> infinite): he may be able to avoid hitting the singularity and
> instead fall thorough a 'wormhole' and come out in another
> region of the universe. This would offer great possibilities for
> travel in space and time, but unfortunately it seems that these
> solutions may all be highly unstable; the least disturbance, such
> as the presence of an astronaut, may change them so that the
> astronaut could not see the singularity until he hit it and his time
> came to an end. In other words, the singularity would always lie
> in his future and never in his past. The strong version of the
> cosmic censorship hypothesis states that in a realistic solution
> the singularities would always lie entirely in his future (like the
> singularities of gravitational collapse), or entirely in the past (like
> the big bang). It is greatly to be hoped that some version of the
> censorship hypothesis holds because close to naked singularities
> it may be possible to travel into the past. While this would be
> fine for writers of science fiction, it would mean that no one's
> life would ever be safe; someone might go into the past and kill
> your father or mother before you were conceived. [Hawking said
> that cosmic censorship might be paraphrased as 'God abhors a
> naked singularity'.]
>
> (1988: 89)

Professor Hawking concluded from all this that 'we find ourselves in a bewildering world'. We certainly do.

In everyday life we experience the flow of time, and therefore may
feel that the views of the physicists I will quote do not really concern
us, but in considering the cases set out in this book we should
remember that the people described as experiencing the past in the
present were almost certainly in an altered state of consciousness,
and although such an experience may not have happened to us
we should not assume that it cannot happen to others. In his
important book *The Emperor's New Mind* (1990) Roger Penrose,

a distinguished physicist and mathematician who is Rouse Ball Professor of Mathematics at Oxford University, suggests that we may be going badly wrong if we apply the usual physical rules for *time* when we consider consciousness:

> The whole of space-time must be fixed, without any scope for uncertainty. . . . Moreover, there is no flow of time at all. We just have 'space-time' – and no scope at all for a future whose domain is being inexorably encroached upon by a determined past. . . . It seems to me that there are several discrepancies between what we consciously feel, concerning the flow of time, and what our (marvellously accurate) theories assert about the reality of the physical world. These discrepancies must surely be telling us something deep about the physics that must presumably actually underlie our conscious perception.
>
> (1990: 393-394)

It should not be necessary to point out that once we have granted that time does not flow in the way we have been accustomed to think that it does, we should not be too surprised that retrocognitive experiences can occur to someone in an altered state of consciousness.

Dr John Beloff, who until recently was senior lecturer in psychology at Edinburgh University and is a former president of the Society for Psychical Research (SPR), points out in a recent book, *The Relentless Quest: Reflections on the Paranormal* (1990), that it has been widely held by parapsychologists that extra-sensory perception (ESP) is essentially independent of space, time and matter, so that when we use our extra-sensory powers instead of relying on our sensory channels and their associated brain mechanisms there is no inherent reason why we should not become as much aware of events occurring in the past or the future as of events occurring contemporaneously, just as there is no inherent reason why we should not become aware of events occurring in remote places or events shielded from us by intervening matter.

Dr Beloff thought it would be very odd if psychokinesis (PK), the direct influence of mind on a physical system without the mediation of any known physical energy, behaved in this respect any differently from ESP, considering that the two are so closely linked that it is customary to subsume both phenomena under the generic term *psi*. The problem of demonstrating forward PK was exactly matched by the problem of demonstrating backward PK, otherwise known as retrocognition, Beloff said. In the latter case, although the subject's response could be recorded prior to verification, the verification would not be possible but for the existence of certain records in the present. Hence, there could be no unequivocal test of retrocognition. Fortunately, there was no such logical barrier in the way of demonstrating unequivocally the existence of a backward or retroactive PK.

Dr Beloff gives details of such an experiment carried out by an American scientist, Dr Helmut Schmidt, who used as his target system a device known as a random number generator. A prominent feature of the Schmidt setup was a feedback system. Beloff maintains that if we adopt the Schmidt axiom that all *psi* interactions depend critically on feedback, then ESP too involves backward causation, proceeding from the moment at which the feedback is received to the earlier moment in time at which the response was given.

John Beloff states that 'the idea of backward causation, so far from being nonsensical, is now taken seriously by more and more experimenters as a basis for testing *psi* in the laboratory'.

A leading British scientist who takes the idea of backward causation seriously is Dr Paul Davies, Professor of Theoretical Physics at the University of Newcastle upon Tyne, who said in his book *God and the New Physics* that there are a number of theories in modern physics that involve retroactive causation. The passage reads as follows:

> If time really did have a beginning, any attempt to explain it in terms of causes must appeal to a wider concept of cause than that familiar to us in daily life. One possibility is to relax the requirement that cause always precedes effect. Is it possible for causes to act backwards in time, to produce prior effects? Of course, the idea of changing the past is replete with paradox. Suppose you could influence nineteenth-century events in such a way as to prevent your own birth, for example? Nevertheless there are a number of theories in modern physics that involve retro-active causation. Hypothetical faster-than-light particles (called tachyons) could accomplish this. To avoid paradox, one might suppose that the link between cause and effect is very loose and uncontrollable, or else it is of a more subtle variety.

As we shall see, the quantum theory requires a sort of reversed time causality, inasmuch as an observation performed today can contribute to the construction of reality in the remote past. This point has been emphasized by the physicist John Wheeler: 'The quantum principle shows that there is a sense in which what the observer will do in the future defines what happens in the past – even in a past so remote that life did not then exist'.

(1983: 39)

All this sounds very complex, as indeed it is, and we find ourselves considering some very paradoxical situations in which the past can, in theory, be re-created, although the physicists I have quoted do not use the term ESP. What they do do is to admit the possibility of what the parapsychologists call retrocognition but without being able to give examples of it. The importance of this book, I claim, is in being able, for the first time, to present enough examples of retrocognition to carry conviction, even for the sceptic unless his or her mind is completely closed to the possibility that such phenomena can occur. For such the barrier is psychological rather than one of evidence.

In the cases that follow we have examples of retrocognition taken from real life. Some raise questions by those involved in the experience that cannot at present be answered. For instance, in Chapter 1 William Laing wonders what would have happened if he had knocked on the door of a seemingly empty cottage at Kersey and asks: 'Who might have answered it? It doesn't bear thinking about.' Similarly, a schoolboy, John Watson, who had an experience of a vanished street in Nottingham (Chapter 2), asks: 'What would have happened had I walked further into the street? Would I have passed temporarily into the past or would I have been likely to walk into any present-day obstruction without seeing it?' It is tempting to toy with the idea that some cases of unsolved disappearances might involve people who walked unknowingly into, say, a house that once stood on a site and were swallowed up in the past of the spectral dwelling.

In the two cases I have just quoted there are evidential features I will discuss. However, other cases, equally vivid, cannot be assessed as carefully because they were unaccompanied by evidential features. One such was related to me by the late Lady Carson of Cleve Court, Thanet, Kent, who heard it from the family doctor, the late Dr E. G. Moon, of Broadstairs. Dr Moon also related it to Sir Patrick Macrory, who at the time was tutor to the Carsons' son, Edward. Dr Moon did not want an account of his experience to appear during his lifetime, fearing, naturally, that his patients might mistrust a doctor given to 'seeing things'.

Dr Moon told how, one day in 1930, he had been asked to call on Lord Carson and, after attending him, paused at the front door, looking down, while he considered whether he should have prescribed a stronger tonic. When he looked up a totally different scene from what had been there when he arrived was before his eyes. His car, which had been standing in the small drive before the house, had vanished, as had the thick hedge which is between the two sets of gateposts. Instead of the lane which he had driven down that day there was a muddy track. Coming towards him was a man who was wearing a coat with many capes, a short top hat, and gaiters at which he flicked noiselessly with a hunting-crop.

The man stared at Dr Moon who, not believing the evidence of his eyes, decided to go back into the house. Then he resolved to have another look from the doorway. When he did so the car was where he had left it, the scenery of the present day was restored, and there was no sign of the man who had stared so intently at him. There are a number of accounts in the history of psychical research of incidents in which the action of looking away from an apparition for a second or two causes the figure to disappear. The explanation for this, I believe, is that the decision to look away causes a change in the state of consciousness sufficient to alter what is observed.

Readers will note that in the opening chapter I have given, in what many will consider to be unnecessary detail, facts about the difference between the Kersey of medieval times and the Kersey of today. The reason for this is that an account of a case as important as this will be scrutinized by sceptics in the hope of detecting flaws in it so that it may be discounted. If, for instance, the three youths approaching the village in 1957 were guided by the sound of bells, presumably those of the parish church, which was then visible to them, and it could be proved that the bells were not in operation at the time, this would be judged sufficient cause to dismiss the whole reported experience on the grounds that if this one detail was wrong so, presumably, were others, and the whole narrative was therefore suspect. I took care to check that bells in the church tower were in operation in 1957. Also, and more important, if my statement that no medieval document exists showing that a butcher's shop stood on the site where the three youths said they saw one was proved to be wrong because a scholar produced an early map of the village showing a butcher's shop on another site, then this would be considered a serious flaw in the narrative, casting doubt on the whole case. I therefore had to take the greatest care to ensure that no documentary sources were left unexamined. This involved visits to the library of the University of Cambridge, which holds medieval documents relating to the village, where the University once held land, and to the Suffolk Record Office, to check documentary source. The barrage of arguments used against Miss Moberly's and Miss Jourdain's accounts of what they saw in the park at Versailles in August 1901, and during later visits, prepared me for what I am convinced will be an assault by critics against my account of the Kersey case. If this is thought a needless fear, in view of the weight of evidence I will produce, let me quote a review by Dr Bob Brier, of the Department of Philosophy of Long Island University, of Brian Inglis's book *The Hidden Power* (*Journal of the American Society for Psychical Research*, July 1991); in this review he says that Inglis chronicles a considerable number of attempts to dispose of parapsychological phenomena and he (the reviewer) concludes from this that 'what emerges is that, indeed, there must be something threatening about *psi* phenomena that leads to such frantic, strong and sustained attempts at debunking the field. If this is true, then the real problem is not a scientific one, not one of evidence, not one of finding the repeatable experiment, etc. – it is a psychological one, and one that will not go away quickly'.

In the cases that follow the reader will find some in which belief is strained because they conflict with our ideas of what constitutes space and time and, indeed, reality, but they should not be dismissed from consideration for that reason. Instead they should cause us to ponder on the nature of reality and of our relation to the universe. I regret that I have been unable to offer a larger number of examples of ostensible retrocognition but, as Dr Gauld pointed out in his Introduction, they are 'fascinating, exceedingly rare and very hard to evaluate'. I hope in due course, with the help of readers, to present a larger selection.

PART ONE

Three youths in a medieval village, the Versailles 'adventure' and other brushes with the past

Chapter 1

Three Youths in a Medieval Village

It was a beautiful Sunday morning after a cold autumn night in October 1957 when three youths from the Royal Navy shore training establishment, HMS *Ganges*, at Shotley, Suffolk, approached the little village of Kersey in the same county, guided by bells in the course of a training exercise, but on entering the village they saw it as it probably was in medieval times instead of as it is in the twentieth century.

When they entered a lane leading to the southern end of the village the ancient Saxon church, rebuilt by the Normans, which they had glimpsed through trees as they approached across the fields, was no longer visible, hidden behind trees on the mound on which it stands, and they were walking in silence as the bells had abruptly stopped after they climbed a fence a hundred yards from the church. As they turned the corner of a leafy lane they saw, sloping downwards, a dirt track completely empty of houses on the right-hand side, only forest trees, and on the left-hand side two or three houses widely spaced. The track ran down to a stream and then rose to the northern end of the village; here there were more houses and they were small, old and dirty. The youths, all aged 15, could not but notice that instead of there being groups of people chatting in the street, or on their way to church (although the church was no longer visible), the village was completely deserted. The only signs of life were provided by a number of ducks, silent and motionless, by the stream that ran through the centre of the village. Nowhere were there cars, telephone wires, TV and radio aerials, or other indications of contemporary life in the country.

Depression set in as the youths experienced the deathly silence, unbroken by birdsong, that enveloped the village. The world they had left behind them seemed far away as they squatted by the

3

stream, drinking from it to refresh their thirst, and surveyed the empty street. Not even a dog was in sight nor did they feel a breath of wind; no leaves stirred on the tall trees around them. It was, as one of them said afterwards, as if they had stepped back in time. Even the season had changed. Although the fields they had left had the colours of autumn, trees in the village had the fresh greenness of spring.

Jumping the narrow stream, the youths peered into the window of a butcher's shop in which skinned oxen carcasses, green with age, were hanging. This was the only shop visible in the village, and it was so dirty, and festooned with cobwebs, that it suggested the butcher had shut up shop and gone away weeks before. The youths looked into other buildings through windows which were without curtains but it was into rooms bare of furniture. There were no window-boxes bright with flowers, no gardens in front.

By this time the feeling of uneasiness which had been experienced very strongly beside the stream had increased; the youths felt they were surrounded by invisible watchers. Their pace grew faster as they went up the village street and eventually they took to their heels. After turning a corner at the top of the street, they paused to take breath and look back. The silence was now broken by the sound of church bells, smoke hung in the air that in the village had been crystal clear, and behind the trees at the southern end of the village the church was visible.

This extraordinary story, unique in modern times, was contained in a letter dated 20 July 1988 from Mr William Laing, a retired Royal Navy wireless operator, who emigrated to Australia in 1968 and with his wife established a successful business there. He had read an appeal for case material in my book *Hauntings and Apparitions* (London, 1982) and decided to write to me with an account of the Kersey experience and another of an encounter with an apparition in Scotland. Strangely enough, another member of the party, Mr Michael Crowley, had also emigrated to Australia, in 1983, but they have never met there; their last meeting was in Malta in 1963. However, they were in touch occasionally by telephone, Mr Laing living in Leuras, New South Wales, and Mr Crowley in Adelaide, South Australia.

The third member of the party that went to Kersey, Mr Ray Baker, of London, was traced with difficulty, the Admiralty record office being unable to supply his address, but fortunately he

4

responded to an appeal by me in *Navy News*. While Mr Laing had a clear recollection of events in 1957, and Mr Crowley a partial one, Mr Baker seemed to remember little.

Mr Laing was an excellent correspondent, bringing to light details of his experience in an exchange of letters that extended over two years. During this time I made several visits to the village and was fortunate to have the help of Mr Leslie Cockayne, a member of an old Kersey family and an ex-librarian who had made a study of the history of the village. In September 1990 Mr Laing visited the village and walked through it with me, Dr Hugh Pincott (former Hon. Secretary of the Society for Psychical Research) and Mr Cockayne, dictating his impressions on a tape-recorder.

Research, described below, indicates that the Kersey Mr Laing and his companions saw on that autumn day in 1957 fitted with what it could have been in the mid-fifteenth century, a gap of some five hundred years.

The evidence of the principal witnesses follows.

MR LAING'S NARRATIVE

The following account of Mr Laing's experience was compiled by me from many letters written between 1988 and 1990. It incorporates some minor corrections made as a result of questions I raised. His own words are used throughout.

In October 1957 whilst a boy in HMS *Ganges* my class (no. 262, Rodney Division) was sent on a weekend survival exercise, so to speak. This involved spending the night in a barn and afterwards we were split into groups with orders to find our way to different destinations. My group consisted of three, Ray Baker, Michael Crowley and myself. We were boy entrants and had been only seven months in the Service at the time. On a Sunday morning, a beautiful, clear, crisp day, our little group was ordered to find its way to the village or township of Kersey in Suffolk, over the fields on foot, then reporting all we saw within five hours.

We made our way across fields, never by road, or at least only to cross a roadway, then back to the fields and hedgerows. Strangely enough, I caught a large hare in one field. He was flopped down in a lump of long grass. I was surprised that the animal showed no signs of struggle, so instead of killing him for the pot we released him. The only way we caught hares in Scotland was by shooting or dogs.

Shortly afterwards we approached a greyish stone cottage surrounded by large trees, probably oaks, where an obvious farm labourer, his wife and family, stood behind the wall and gate. He eyed us suspiciously and would not have spoken unless we hadn't asked them in what direction Kersey lay. The man pointed and sullenly said 'Hold in that direction' which we did, but his obvious suspicion and attitude affected us because I recall us commenting on it.

It was very shortly afterwards, perhaps ten minutes or so, we saw and heard Kersey on our right-hand side. I can see clearly in my mind's eye the view and position of the roofs and church spire [actually a tower] of Kersey just before we entered the lane from the fields. As we approached from the fields we could hear church bells ringing on our right.

After we had climbed an iron fence from the fields, perhaps 100 yards from the church, the bells abruptly cut out. We seemed to enter a little laneway with extremely ancient houses, almost medieval in appearance, on one side of the lane, which had a strong brown earthen surface, with lots of dust, almost like an Australian stony bush track. I was acutely aware of the silence, probably more so than the others. Whenever I'm in the countryside I'm always on the lookout for birds and animals, being a keen birdwatcher, but there were no calls from either a rook or a blackbird. Nothing, not even a dog to check us out. We were looking for people to greet and give information but there were none. This section of the lane was tree-lined, with greenish-tinged light, but there were few houses. As we moved down the lane I remember the prickly depressing feeling which prevailed. A stream crossed the lane, with a bridge over it near the centre. It consisted of four posts and two wooden planks and a hand-rail, and was about 3 feet high. A cart or vehicle could ford the stream easily; the scene was most picturesque. We squatted or sat here for about ten minutes, drank from the stream and looked around. There was no sign of a church. I would certainly have seen it as I had a field of observation of 360°. Silent ducks sat beside the stream, which was 5 or 6 inches deep, maybe a bit less. The ducks were so quiet and motionless they could have been decoys. This stillness was most apparent to me, as ducks are most active birds. They took no notice of our presence.

Our feelings of unease really started when we sat or squatted by that bridge. The trees were sharply etched against the sky in this particular area, no sound of birds, no wind. The trees burn a hole in my memory and I do remember there being almost a dark hole in the sky, absolutely still and unnatural. Not even a leaf moved. The sky was intensely blue. [When I quoted to Mr Laing Miss Moberly's description of the trees in the park at Versailles on 10 August 1901 being 'flat and lifeless, like a wood worked in tapestry' he replied that this was 'spot on', adding that at Kersey there was no breath of wind, no sound, and there was a definite absence of shadow.]

There was a wide bare area on both sides of the lane south of the stream. One thing I remember is jumping across the stream and remarking how silly it was to build a footbridge across such a shallow narrow stream, but as the water passed under the bridge it appeared dark and there were more ducks there. A few yards from the little wooden bridge [this was on the right-hand side of the lane which went up the hill] there was a butcher's shop, the only commercial building we saw in the village. All three members of the party saw it. There were no tables or counters [in the shop], just two or three whole oxen carcasses which had been skinned and in places were quite green with age. There was a green-painted door and windows with smallish glass panes, one at the front and one at the side, rather dirty-looking. I remember that as we three looked through that window in disbelief at the streaked and mouldy green carcasses I had a strong feeling of unreality, the dirty room, cobwebs, etc., and there was one comment I do recall when someone (it may have been me) said, 'What a waste.' The general feeling certainly was one of disbelief and unreality. The green sheen on the carcasses was almost an iridescent green, perhaps a trick of the light, as it was a brilliant sunny day in 1957, very warm, very still, after a night of frost. One thing it could not have been and that was a phantom building as we would have been leaning against the window-frame as we peered in. The carcasses could have all the appearance of theatrical props but of course they were not. Who would believe in 1957 that the health authorities would allow such conditions, as responsible citizens would have reported them. There was certainly no smell, and on a still day one might think strong smells might issue from under the door. The window was closed, and to all appearances the owner had shut up shop weeks before, leaving the carcasses to rot.

So, Sunday morning on a beautiful clear sunny day in a laneway full of homes, no people, dogs, nobody going to church or chatting by their doorways. If there were any gardens they must have been to the rear of the houses, which were very old in appearance and not detached. When one walks past homes, especially in a neighbourhood like that, one sees evidence of wallpaper or flower vases in windows, etc., but in the laneway the windows in every house reflected back darkly except for one where there was a whitish-coloured wall showing inside, but the window-panes were too small to see through properly and mostly greenish in hue. We looked through windows, or at least a window, and I clearly remember a smallish room with a rear window. There was no furniture inside, no curtains, the white paintwork was dingy and had the appearance of being flat white, either a distemper or whitewash, certainly not of modern-day quality. There was also a staircase on the right-hand side of the room and I clearly remember seeing the side and bottom panels of the staircase, also a dull white colour. Incidentally, the front door led straight into that room and one would have virtually entered under the staircase. There were no gardens in front of the houses, no electrical wires or antennae. That butcher's shop was the only business we saw. It was a ghost village, so to speak. I experienced an overwhelming feeling of sadness and depression in Kersey but also a feeling of unfriendliness and unseen watchers which sent shivers up one's back, a strange eerie sadness I'll never forget and a silence out of this world.

Imagine that beautiful Sunday morning in 1957 – three 15-year-olds full of excitement away from the routine of *Ganges*. I was enjoying the sun and fresh air, trees and fields, then suddenly Kersey and that eerie sadness. Something certainly happened to make us feel that way. I maintain the place felt quite evil and hostile to us. I am a Highlander, grew up in the wilds of Perthshire, very close to the land. I have always lived close to nature and have seen quiet days but never a still quiet such as at Kersey. I would have to notice the strange silence. I wouldn't miss the sounds of nature; my whole being was programmed to them. I was a very fine poacher in Scotland as a boy and one had to be aware of sounds and the presence of people around. Mike Crowley is also a country boy, from Wiltshire, but Ray Baker is a Cockney and it probably didn't occur to him that something was wrong, but I do remember we all felt it in the end and took to our heels.

There is one obvious point I've missed, the autumn colour of the grass and vegetation as we approached the village, but it was verdant in Kersey along from the bridge, and the trees were that magnificent green one finds in spring or early summer. Could we have walked from autumn to spring in ten minutes? I'm certain of that autumn grass colour outside the village and the spring hue in Kersey. There is a different light in spring and autumn and I am very conscious of colour and light. When I was a boy in Perthshire I loved the fresh spring colour of larch and beech and oak and the colour that filtered through trees, the same as in the laneway in 1957.

There were few houses before the stream but more afterwards. I seem to remember a house with a sculpture or gargoyle above the door but it's a vague memory. If there had been wires, either telephone or electric, radio or TV aerials, I'd have seen them because at the time it was painfully obvious there were none, or street-lights, etc. – nothing at all.

The little lane narrowed and the houses were closer together, almost suffocating one – not a sound or person, the only sign of life the white ducks. We hurried out of the lane then suddenly we could hear the bells once more and saw smoke rising from chimneys, but none of the chimneys was smoking when we were in the village. When we left the laneway and entered the fields to the west we ran for a few hundred yards as if to shake off the weird feeling.

It was almost as if we'd walked back in time. I can still feel the uneasiness, fear and depression we felt in 1957. I wonder if we'd knocked at a door to ask a question who might have answered it? It doesn't bear thinking about.

The whole round trip was possibly no more than two hours or so, perhaps two and a half. On reporting the details to the petty officer in charge, he was rather sceptical but laughed it off about the hare incident and agreed we'd seen Kersey all right.

9

Mr Laing ended his first letter with the comment that 'This was thirty years ago and perhaps you have other references to this in your archives. Perhaps there is a perfectly logical explanation, but it is extremely odd that in an English lane with lots of houses we never saw a soul.'

He estimated that the group was in the village for twenty-five or thirty minutes.

MR MICHAEL CROWLEY'S ACCOUNT

I received only one letter from Mr Michael Crowley about his experience at Kersey. This was sent to me in December 1988. He started by saying that he had spoken over the telephone to Mr Laing about it and that quite a bit of what he (Mr Laing) related he could not remember; Mr Laing's recollections did not jog his memory. He went on to say:

> I do still remember basically that it was something unusual that we both had seen . . . . As I remember it would have been around November time 1957 when we were at HMS *Ganges*, Shotley, Suffolk. Our class (no. 262) was scheduled to go on a short weekend expedition. We were not informed where we would actually be going. The class (20) left *Ganges* early Saturday afternoon and travelled for about two to three hours towards Ipswich and then through the country roads and lanes. We eventually arrived at a farmyard and were billeted in the barn. The evening and night consisted of the usual meal and get-together.
>
> The night had been cold and on the Sunday morning the sun was shining and there had been a frost, a very crisp sunny morning. When breakfast was over and the barn had been cleaned up we were assembled and then split into groups, our group consisting of three, Bill Laing, Ray Baker (from London) and myself. We were given an assignment which was to head in a certain direction for about 5 miles and report what we had seen on our return. The time would have been around 9 a.m. when we set off as it was still quite cold. As I remember we followed a road for a while and then cut across some fields (why now I cannot recall).

In my mind now I can see down towards a village behind some trees. The time would have been around 12 noon. When we walked into the village the first noticeable thing was there was not anyone around. The village had only one street with houses, very old (reminded me of some villages I had seen in the Cotswolds) and small. The only thing that really sticks in my mind is a butcher's shop with meat still hanging inside which looked as though it had been hanging for a very long time. It is hard now to describe or even remember how I felt. I do remember the suggestion being made that perhaps everyone was at church but there was no church to be seen.

How long we remained I cannot recollect. The whole time in the village not one other person did we see. I remember we talked about what could have happend to all the people and I think from my own point that this was a place that had been evacuated for some reason during the war and had never been resettled. Nevertheless, it was still most unusual what I actually felt, probably disbelief that a place like this existed and had been left untouched (no broken windows, etc.).

Points that I do remember:

Street not overgrown.

Street ran downhill in slight curve to left.

Houses opposite butcher's shop empty (looked in a few).

No aerials, street-lights, telephone wires, posts.

No noise.

No animals.

No church or pub.

That's about all that comes back to mind. I did not know the name of the village we had been to until last year [1987] when I asked Bill if he knew the name. Perhaps I had forgotten after all this time but it came as a surprise that Bill knew.

Being a rather practical person I have never attached any abnormal reason behind what we had seen, just a curiosity as to why it was so. Maybe it was not Kersey that we had been to but a village within that same area. The thing that puzzles me is that as far as we knew no one else knew of this place but then I wonder why we were sent in that direction to report what we had seen if there was nothing to report.

One small thing that does come to mind was that we almost

stepped on a hare when crossing the fields after leaving the village.

I asked Mr Laing for his comments on his companion's doubts on the name of the village they had visited. He replied: 'There is no doubt in my mind we were in Kersey in '57. Just looking at the postcard you posted to me I recognize various typographical features but I definitely can say there were no pubs, cars, cafés, etc., only as I have described. We were definitely there but in God only knows what time.'

THE THIRD WITNESS

The third member of the party was Mr Ray Baker, now a computer operator for an oil company. Mr Laing and Mr Crowley had lost touch with him, as with other members of the course. Attempts to trace him through official channels failed but the helpful suggestion was made that he might reply to a letter in *Navy News*, a periodical circulating in the Service. Fortunately Mr Baker's attention was drawn to this and he telephoned Mr Laing in Australia. However, he could not help with information. Mr Laing wrote to me, 'The terrible thing is that he remembers little or nothing of Kersey village. However, I suppose that going on examples of retrocognition in your book not all people in certain situations experience the same thing.' Mr Baker remembered the night in the barn but that was all. I rang Mr Baker, who admitted: 'I did not notice anything.' I arranged to meet him but due to a misunderstanding on my part this meeting did not eventuate. Mr Laing hoped to meet him when he visited England in September 1990, but for some of that time Mr Baker was abroad on holiday. However, the two men did speak on the telephone without any fresh information on the episode in 1957 coming to light. I think we may take into consideration the possibility that Mr Baker, as a young Londoner, may have had little conception of what a country village in the 1950s was like and would not share the surprise of Mr Laing and Mr Crowley, both country lads. Another factor to be considered is that people vary greatly in sensitivity in their reactions to a place. Mr Laing wrote to me in 1990 from Australia that 'Funnily enough, Kersey feels odd and depressing even after all these years'. However, when he visited the village with me in September 1990, he did not find the experience depressing.

KERSEY IN THE 1990s

The picture of the village as a grubby little place, painted by Mr Laing in his letters, bears little resemblance to the Kersey of the 1990s. When you approach the village you see, visible for miles around, the tall tower of the church, and in the village itself the church is plainly visible, and would be so even had it no tower. Instead of a dirt track through the village there is a paved road. The stream, known locally as the water-splash, is crossed on the eastern side by an attractive footbridge which bears no resemblance to the crude plank-and-post structure spanning it 'near the centre' described by Mr Laing. Poles, wires and TV and radio aerials are everywhere. Extensive 'gentrification' has taken place. Many houses have been painted a warm, shade of pink. Gardens are bright with flowers. There are two public houses, the Bell, which has been much restored, and the White Horse, both with signs hanging outside, a restaurant, a general store, a pottery and a sub-post office. Kersey, tucked away in a fold in the fields, is easily missed, but once inside you can see that it deserves the description of Sir Nikolaus Pevsner in his *The Buildings of England* as 'the most picturesque village of South Suffolk'. Indeed, it is one of the most picturesque in England, attracting visitors from all over the world. As Pevsner points out, 'The view from the church over the tiled roofs of the houses dipping down to the ford [across a tributary] of the River Brett and climbing up on the other side is not easily forgotten. The church lies on its own at the end of the village, which is just one long street with an extension by the stream.' There are still many thatched cottages.

Kersey is certainly very old. Outside two houses in the village, one at the northern end and one near the stream, are the remains of two 'pudding stones' – a large number of flints or pebbles set in a matrix of sandstone – that were markers of a track that ran for nearly 200 miles from the shores of the Wash through East Anglia into Berkshire over five thousand years ago. It is not known if the place was inhabited then. First mentioned in an Anglo-Saxon will of about AD 990, Kersey was already a thriving

community at the time of the Norman Conquest. The Domesday
Book of 1086 describes the village's inhabitants and their farming
activities and mentions a church 'with three acres'. At the time the
Domesday Book was compiled there might have been only half a
dozen cottages in the centre of Kersey.

Kersey is next mentioned a hundred years later in the tax records
of Abbot Sampson of Bury St Edmunds. About this time a local
heiress, Nesta de Cokefield, gave land on the northern side of the
valley for the foundation of an Augustinian priory, followed by the
gift of the advowson of the parish church. This meant that the prior
became responsible for providing priests for the parish.

Meanwhile, the village was growing and seems to have enjoyed
considerable prosperity. The lord of the manor of Kersey was
granted the right to hold a weekly market in 1252, and early in
the following century the church, already rebuilt since Domesday,
was further enlarged. Tradition has it that local wealth was based
on wool exports, but there is no evidence for this, although sheep-
rearing figured prominently in the pattern of farming recorded in
the Domesday Book. On the other hand, cloth-making was well
established by the beginning of the fourteenth century in nearby
towns such as Hadleigh and Sudbury, and there are indications that
Kersey might also have been involved, although the association of
its name with a type of coarse ribbed cloth made up in short and
narrow lengths is not supported by historical evidence.

The development of the village was checked by the Black Death
in 1349. A large proportion of the population died and work on the
enlargement of the church was suspended. The village recovered
during the following century and some of the work on the church
was completed, including the construction of the tower, but the
priory, which had been in financial difficulties for some years,
went into decline and was dissolved in 1444. Its lands passed
eventually to King's College, Cambridge, which also took over the
responsibility for appointing the parish priest. This right was not
relinquished until the 1920s and the college sold its lands in 1930.

By the end of the fifteenth century, cloth-making in Kersey and
neighbouring towns was enjoying a boom which lasted throughout the sixteenth century, but when the centre of the woollen
industry moved north to Yorkshire in the seventeenth century
Kersey became almost entirely dependent on agriculture, and its
population and prosperity rose and fell in line with the fortunes

of that industry. There was a peak in the middle of the nineteenth century, when the population rose to nearly 800, but after the 1870s it fell steadily to its present level of around 350. Now, in the last quarter of the twentieth century, relatively few Kersey people work on the land. Many have jobs in nearby towns and even as far away as London, and there is a large element of retired people.

According to a chronicler in an information sheet in the parish church, the changes in village life over the past 150 years have been particularly marked. In 1844 the population of 787 supported three shoemakers, two tailors, two blacksmiths, two cornmillers, a grocer and draper, a baker, a saddler, a wheelwright, a brewer and several bricklayers and carpenters, as well as two public house, which are still there.

Mr Laing, informed of this, wrote that the Kersey he saw in 1957 could not have supported a population of over 700. In the course of correspondence he drew a sketch map of the village as he remembered it. Wooded areas were shaded green. Among these was the mound on which the church stands, although the church was not indicated. The site of a butcher's shop was indicated on the right-hand side of the track just over the stream. I sent Mr Laing postcards of the village, obtained from the church, and on one of these he marked with arrows the route his party had taken through the village from the direction of the church. This was the first time the route had been made clear to me because before then I had assumed entry had been from the north. Above a house on the northern side of the stream, the first on the right as one goes up the hill, was an arrow with the inscription 'possible site of the butcher's'. On a visit to Kersey in March 1990 I knocked on the door of the house indicated, Bridge House. My knock was answered by the owner, Mrs Jillian Finch. I showed her the marked photograph with some trepidation, thinking it most unlikely that Mr Laing's memory could have been reliable on this point, particularly as Bridge House was an elegant residence. However, Mrs Finch showed no surprise at my question, replying: 'But this used to be a butcher's shop.' I was astonished that Mr Laing's identification had been confirmed.

As the butcher's shop was the only business seen in the village by Mr Laing's little group I set out to investigate the past history of the house. Could it have been marked in any medieval documents? I wrote to Mr A. E. B. Owen, Keeper of Manuscripts at the

University of Cambridge Library, where the papers of King's College relating to the land-holdings are kept, and I followed this up with a personal visit. Mr Owen kindly went through all the papers from medieval times, which included a rent roll for land and houses, to see if there was any reference to a butcher's shop, but the occupations of those who paid rent were not given. Among the documents were a rent roll of Kersey Priory Manor of 1587, again without any indications of where the properties were or the occupations of the owners, and a report of the sitting of the manor court in 1550 for an exchange of holdings. There was no map of the village. Mr Owen pointed out that medieval maps were 'quite rare' and that 'it was most unusual to get maps of small localities before the sixteenth century'. A search for papers relating to Kersey in medieval times at the Bury St Edmunds branch of the Suffolk Record Office was similarly fruitless. Mr Cockayne said that he could not recall any mention of a butcher's shop in any will from the late fifteenth century to the nineteenth, and he had read most of the wills.

However, Mr Cockayne was able to throw light on the history of the building now known as Bridge House from personal knowledge, as it had once been owned by his family. His maternal great-grandfather, Robert Vince, had once run a butchery business from the house, as had his father, also named Robert. They sold cheap joints of meat from the house, but the principal income came from the sale of cattle driven to the London market. The elder Robert Vince's father, James, was also a butcher, but it is not known if he lived in the house, although he probably did. Thus, the house was associated with a butchery business from about 1790 onwards, with the two Robert Vinces, father and son, active between 1840 and 1880.

I discussed the probable age of Bridge House with Mrs Finch and Miss Gladys King, then aged 83, who lived in another part of the building; the two dwellings were joined by a passage. They had been told that the oldest part of the building dated from around 1350. They believed that the butcher's shop had closed about 1905. Earlier I had been told by Mr Jack Stiff, a member of an old Kersey family, that there had been a butcher's shop by the stream at the turn of the century, so some confirmation was available on this point. Miss King said that she had been brought to the house by her family in 1918. The bay window at her end of the house was used as a general store and sweet-shop until the 1970s. Mr Cockayne told me that the closing-down of the butcher's shop would not have involved radical alterations to the building.

Mr Cockayne said that when the bridge over the water-splash was built in the middle of the last century, his ancestor the younger Robert Vince planted a willow tree by the bridge to mark the boundary of his land. The record office contains an account of how this tree was blown down in 1950, destroying the bridge, which had to be replaced. The willow tree that stands by the bridge now is a sapling of the old tree. The year when the tree fell was a crucial one for the village because it was then that running water and electricity were introduced and modernization could begin.

At last the day arrived, after more then two years of correspondence, when I could join Mr Laing on the spot to compare his impressions of Kersey as it was today with those of when he last saw it in 1957. We met on 11 September 1990 in Lavenham, west of Kersey, and drove in Dr Pincott's car to a point where we could enter Kersey from the south, as Mr Laing's little group had done in 1957. We paused within sight of the church, which, Mr Laing pointed out, had been visible to them through trees. At this spot there were large bare fields from which crops had been harvested. Mr Laing said that in 1957 they had approached the village across meadows laced with hedgerows through which they had to force their way. Looking around, he now thought they could have approached the village from the south-east instead of from the south-west, as he had supposed. I thought his view was probably correct, as bells had been heard on their right. Smoke hung over the village then and a few slate roofs could be glimpsed. Mr Cockayne joined us here. We had to decide by which of the two lanes we would enter the village. I selected what seemed to be the older of the two, but as it led directly to the church, and Mr Laing remarked 'We could hardly have avoided seeing that', we retraced our steps. The lane down which we next walked was the one that provided vehicular access to the village. Large bushes on the bank on the right hid the church from view. As we emerged from the lane Mr Laing, indicating the mound on which the church stood, to our right, said, 'There were large trees here.' Now we stood on Church Hill, as the street was called, looking down to the stream at the bottom of the dip. Indicating a row of old cottages on the right, which led to a pottery at the bottom, Mr Laing said, 'None of these were here then, there were only forest trees.' Looking to the left, where again there were rows of cottages, he pointed out that in 1957 this side of the hill contained only two or three cottages, widely spaced apart. The panes of glass in the cottages on the left were, he said, larger than those he had seen here in 1957. One of these cottages could have been Mr Cockayne's, which stood on the site of what was once the village green, a wedge-shaped area.

We paused on the southern side of the water-splash. Indicating a large mass of greenery on his left Mr Laing said, 'This wasn't here then; this place was bare.' It was, in fact, the area where the market was once held. Mr Cockayne had told me earlier than an old document of 1390 concerned the holding of a market here with stalls. One of the buildings facing this area is named Market House, a reminder of those times.

The sight of the stream reminded Mr Laing that when they were last here it had been so hot that they had taken off their jerseys and tied them around their necks. I asked him to indicate where the bridge they had seen had crossed the stream and he indicated a spot on the extreme left of the lane. The banks of the stream to the left were heavily overgrown, he pointed out, more so than when his group was here in 1957. Mr Laing commented on the shallowness of the stream, 'shallow enough for us to wade through it', and said it was wider than when they had crossed by jumping over it in 1957. The water then had ploughed a little channel, whereas now there was a concrete base to the stream, which ran at an angle across the street, as compared with the straight course when they saw it. The willow tree by the bridge was not there, he pointed out. Gazing at the Muscovy ducks, an imported breed, he said that the ducks he had seen were of the native mallard type.

Mr Laing gazed intently to his right where Bridge House, the nearest house to the bridge across the stream, stood. 'That used to be a butcher's shop,' Mr Cockayne said, but Mr Laing remarked, 'That's wrong. There was a bare area in front.' While he pondered this point cars drew up in The Street, as this section of the lane is called, to disgorge children who picked up the little ducklings, which were splashing after their parents. On crossing the water-splash Mr Laing examined the first few houses on the right-hand side as if trying to verify his impression of where the butcher's shop stood, although I had already told him by letter that Bridge House had been identified as occupying the site of the butcher's shop.

Gazing up The Street at the inn signs hanging outside the Bell on the left and the White Horse further up the lane on the right, he asked, 'How could we have missed them?' The White Horse, as I knew from earlier inquiries there, had been established on that spot 450 years ago as a coaching inn, and the Bell was claimed to be 700 years old. It is certainly a very old building, much restored, and is an attraction for tourists.

Mr Laing, I knew, was looking for a building with a green door and green window-sills, such as he remembered the butcher's shop having, and was excited when he detected fragments of green paint in the window-sill of the restaurant opposite the Bell and was told that the door had once been painted green. However, he concluded that this building was too far up the street to have been the butcher's shop, and his attention was again drawn to the houses near the stream. Although it was now past lunch time, we did not want to interrupt Mr Laing's flow of impressions as he tried to recover what he had remembered of the past, and we continued up The Street. Mr Laing thought that the lane had seemed narrower then, with overhanging buildings, and he appeared puzzled by a large patch of greenery in a break in the row of houses on the left. Mr Cockayne told him that houses had once stood there but had been destroyed, he believed, eighty or ninety years ago. Buildings at this point, we considered, would, if overhanging, make the lane seem narrower. A few days later Mr Laing rang me to say that the sculpture or gargoyle he seemed to remember being on a building could have been on one in this stretch of The Street.

As we neared the top of the lane Mr Laing remarked that he remembered seeing some paving-stones, about 18 inches square, standing in the earth track here. We left the village by a road which turned to the right at the top. As we paused there, Mr Laing said that this was the point at which the bells cut in again when his group was there in 1957. Then they had seen the church and the pall of smoke hanging over the village. While they were in the village the air had been crystal clear.

In this account there are several pointers to the time to which Mr Laing's experience could apply. The most significant relates to the church and the tower. The building of the tower was halted by the Black Death in 1349, with the walls built up to the first string-course (a projecting course running along the face of a building); an architect told me that I could assume this would be between 8 and 15 feet high. Work restarted in the fifteenth century, and the tower was completed about 1481. I feel we cannot assume that Mr Laing's experience relates to a time earlier than the fifteenth century because he had a clear recollection of cottages with small panes of glass with a greenish hue. Such glass was not available for domestic use in the fourteenth century. Even as late as the sixteenth century panes were still very small owing to the size of glass available. Glass was in fairly general use in the fifteenth century, although poorer cottages continued to have wooden shutters to keep out the cold at night in place of glass. I had some doubts about whether cottages in a remote country village such as Kersey would have glass windows at a time when the tower was being built but Mr Cockayne assured me that because of the prosperity from cloth one could expect windows to be extensively glazed. Mr Laing's party gazed through windows into bare rooms. According to an authoritative source (I consulted *The English Home* by Doreen Yarwood, London, 1974), in the fourteenth century there was little or no furniture in the average poor country cottage: possessions were kept in baskets or boxes. The same could also apply to the following century. Taking all these factors into consideration, and bearing in mind that the mound on which the church stood was heavily wooded, as Mr Laing remembers, it seems that the experience of his group relates to a time when the tower was under construction but not yet completed, possibly between 1420 and 1460. At that time the tower could still be hidden behind trees. When completed it would thrust above the trees. In one of his letters Mr Cockayne wrote that 'There are several mentions in wills 1470–1500 of benefactions towards the building of the church tower. Thus for most of the fifteenth century there was no tower or in its incomplete state it did not rise to visibility from a distance.'

Although I had been corresponding with Mr Laing for more than two years, as I have explained, and his letters were packed with detailed information, mostly in reply to questions I had asked, I waited until his arrival before drafting this chapter because it is rash to attempt to assess the evidence in a case concerning retrocognition without taking into consideration *all* the evidence and not only that which fits some theory the writer may have evolved. Initially, I was tempted to think that Mr Laing and his companions saw the village as it was at the time of the Black Death (1349), when work on the tower was suspended, but I rejected this because windows in a country cottage would not have been glazed then. I always had in mind the thought that Miss Moberly and Miss Jourdain would not have landed themselves in the trouble they had with their critics if they had kept an open mind about the period to which their experiences related and they had not been so obsessed, on slender evidence, with 1789 and the fate of Marie Antoinette. It is clear, when reading *An Adventure* today, that much of their 'Results of Research', to which they devoted so much time, is of little value because it was irrelevant.

I had formed some impressions of what Kersey could have been like in medieval times from my visits to the village, but it was not until I went there with Mr Laing that I grasped the significance of certain points about which until then I had been undecided. The principal one was whether the mound on which the church stood could have been so heavily wooded as to obscure the church from a point below it. It was not until Mr Laing had pointed out on the spot that the entire right-hand side of the lane before the stream was empty of houses and occupied by 'forest trees' that I realized that neighbouring woodlands had infringed on the village and that trees on the mound could have been large enough to obscure the church from the gaze of observers at the stream, looking upwards. There is some evidence that there were still woods in that vicinity at a much later date because when I visited the Cambridge University Library Mr Owen produced a document relating to the sale of a wood in the vicinity (unnamed) in 1751.

Two of the accounts mention the butcher's shop and the decaying meat in it and point out that there was no church or pub, which there certainly were in 1957; indeed the church, with its tower, dominates the village. The Bell was certainly there in the 1400s but probably not as an inn. I was unable to establish how long it had been licensed but was told that it had temporarily lost its licence three hundred years ago; possibly the licence had been granted a short time before then. The landlord of the White Horse claimed to have the oldest licensed premises in the village.

Two of the youths said that they did not see any overhead wires. According to Mr Cockayne, prior to the 1950s there were a few telephone wires in the village.

Mr Laing and his companions probably approached Kersey shortly before 11 a.m. when bells in the church tower there were ringing for the morning service. Mr Cockayne pointed out to me that 'the youths could have approached Kersey through meadows to the east in 1957. Kersey, like Lavenham, still has vistas which could appear to a townsman as medieval.' Two of the youths, however, were raised in the country.

Mr Laing mentioned a number of times during our visit that the lane he saw in 1957 was narrower than it is today, particularly on the northern side of the stream. If we assess the fifteenth century as the period to which the youths' experience applies there were certainly buildings standing then which are still there today, so the width of the street would be the same. I feel that on this one point he could be mistaken. In a letter written in 1990 he said: 'over the course of our communication I've always kept in mind that the mind can play tricks and have had to keep from self-influence and stick by everything I remember'. He was also uncertain about the route by which we had entered the village. In his first letter after his return to Australia he wrote: 'I feel there must have been an older lane which led into the lane (Church Hill) where Mr Cockayne's house is. Remember I said we turned right and entered the village.' Indeed I do remember Mr Laing saying this. He searched assiduously in the area leading to the site of the old market-place to see if he could find such a route. By the present route from the south one turns left into Church Hill, not right.

Mr Laing's memory of what he saw in 1957 was accurate on a number of important points, which is unusual when the events of a single visit to a village more than thirty years earlier are recalled. In one letter he said, 'Quite often I have surprised people with my good memory and also I am an extremely observant person. Little actually escapes my notice.' He placed accurately on a sketch map of the village sent from Australia the position of the butcher's shop, stated correctly that in early times there were more houses on the northern side of the stream than on the southern, that houses had once stood in a section of the lane on the northern side of the stream that is now bare, and that there had once been a bridge across the stream very different from the one there today and almost certainly in a different position. Mr Cockayne told me that a bridge was mentioned in a late-fifteenth-century will.

However, one important piece of evidence is missing: that the building now known as Bridge House was a butcher's shop in medieval times. Searches of medieval documents in Cambridge by Mr Owen and by Mr Cockayne in Kersey have not brought this information to light and, in all probability, no such document exists. There certainly would be a butcher's shop in a medieval village where a great deal of meat and fish was eaten by the well-to-do. Cattle were killed off each autumn since there were no root crops, although there was cheese, eggs, fruit, vegetables and coarse oatcakes. It is known there was a slaughter house behind what is now Bridge House when it was used as a butchery business, and I do not think it is unreasonable to suppose that probably the village butchery had always been conducted from the same premises. It is unlikely that a village as small as Kersey in medieval times could have had two butchers' shops. The building concerned dates back to the fifteenth century, it has the necessary facilities for conducting a butchery business, such as a slaughter house at the back, and when one family gave up the business it could have been taken over by another family. Any critic who finds this argument unconvincing has to explain away as coincidence the fact that Mr Laing, in Australia, where he had no access to East Anglian research facilities, was able to indicate accurately on a postcard showing a street scene in Kersey a building from which a butchery business was once conducted, probably as far back as 1790, or even earlier.

Other points of criticism will undoubtedly arise so let me antici-pate them and deal with them one by one.

The first is the usual one that a report of the experience was not written down at the time. I raised this point with Mr Laing and his answer was that it never occurred to him to do so. However, he had incorporated a brief report on the Kersey incident in an account of his training at HMS *Ganges* written in 1975. The youths probably thought that by giving an account of their experience to their petty officer they had fulfilled their duty; in any event, it is likely that the concentrated training they were undergoing at a naval training establishment left them very tired at the end of the day and with little inclination for writing.

The second and, in my opinion, more valid objection is that people cannot remember accurately events of thirty years earlier and that distortion of memory is bound to occur. Therefore, accounts of such events should be treated with reservation. I agree up to a point, but against this view it may be argued that some events are so extraordinary that they are remembered for a lifetime and may be recalled in detail.

A third point of criticism could be that the two witnesses in the Kersey experience talked it over between themselves before committing each account to writing and therefore those accounts did not truly represent an individual viewpoint. As a result, the value of such testimony is diminished. In the case under review we should bear in mind that the reports came from two people living hundreds of miles apart in Australia who had not met since 1963. Their only contact was by telephone. In such circumstances it is difficult to concoct a story. It was not until 1987 that, during a talk over the telephone, Mr Crowley remarked to Mr Laing, 'Hey, do you remember that weird village?' This set Mr Laing's mind to work and, as a result of reading one of my books, he decided to write to me. He mentioned that in one of their occasional talks over the telephone Mr Crowley had described Kersey 'as though it was a Hollywood film set of a medieval village which had been left standing'.

Could Mr Laing's group have gone to some other village in the area with a stream running through it but without a church? This possibility must certainly be kept in mind – it occurred to me – but it will not bear close analysis. The youths were directed to the village by a man they met on their way to it and the church was visible on their approach to the village and also after they had left it. Mr Laing recognized certain features of the village from pictures even before returning there and, as he pointed out to me, what other village could there be in the area with no people in sight, no indications of modern life, and with a butcher's shop so dirty, and with decaying meat in it, that any local council would close it down? Also, as Mr Cockayne said to me, 'Nowhere else in Suffolk is there a village with the characteristics of Kersey.'

Could Mr Laing's account have been influenced by something he had read about Kersey? It does not seem so. I was told in the library of the neighbouring town of Hadleigh that 'Unfortunately there is almost no printed history about the place [Kersey], as is so often the case with small villages' and this was confirmed by Mr Cockayne. However, there is a printed information sheet giving the history of the village in the parish church; but is is very unlikely that this would be available in Australia.

Finally, we come to the most commonly used criticism of accounts of spontaneous cases, which is that unless they can be ascribed to lapses of memory, malobservation, misinterpretation of

natural phenomena, etc., they can be attributed to fraud. Therefore, in this case, Mr Laing and Mr Crowley in Australia could
have put their heads together and decided to tell a 'tall story' to
an author in England to see if he would swallow it. Let us assume,
for the sake of argument, that this was so. Certain difficulties
would arise in carrying out the plot as everything would have
to be arranged by telephone. Mr Crowley was absent for days
at a time because he was engaged in a transport business carrying
supplies to another part of the state. However, they did manage
to make contact occasionally by telephone. If they had managed
to concoct a story, then surely they would tell the same story.
When we examine the narratives we find important differences.
Mr Laing said that the field exercise took place in October; Mr
Crowley gives the month as 'around November'. Mr Laing said
that the group was directed to the village by the man standing
outside his cottage; Mr Crowley does not mention this. Mr Laing
said they caught a hare on the way to the village; Mr Crowley
said it was after they had left the village. Critics often point to
inconsistencies in accounts of the same experience as a reason
for classifying them as unreliable and therefore to be dismissed.
My view, based on long experience, is that we should beware of
stories that agree in every particular, as this could be the result of
collusion. Mr Laing did not know what Mr Crowley had written
until we met in England. People remember things differently and
can be expected to differ about details. What we need to look for,
I suggest, is agreement on the main points, and this agreement is
shown by the fact that they both said there was no church visible
from the stream once they were in the village, and no pub, there
was a butcher's shop with decaying meat in it, there were none of
the features that could be found in any country village in England
in the 1950s, and not a person or animal was seen, apart from
the ducks (mentioned only by Mr Laing). Mr Laing answered
all the points I raised promptly and in detail and was willing to
be interrogated in depth over a long period. He impressed me as
being a person of integrity and of strong principles. Nor did he seem
to be credulous. In his first letter he said: 'Let me say that for a long
time I have been sceptical of so-called hauntings by apparitions with
any obvious intelligence and have maintained that apparitions exist
but only in that they are the remains of a past energy perhaps trig-
gered off by meteorological conditions such as static electricity.'

In the account of her second visit to the Petit Trianon in January 1902, Miss Jourdain wrote of how, when she was crossing a bridge to go to the Hameau, 'the old feeling returned in full force; it was as if I had crossed a line and was suddenly in a circle of influence'. This phrase appealed to Mr Laing when I drew his attention to it. His little group entered their circle of influence as they climbed over the fence before entering the village, when the bells cut out, and they were confined in it, in a state of hallucination, until they left at the northern end, some twenty-five or thirty minutes later, when the bells were heard again. During this period of hallucination the scenery of the present day was obliterated and that of an earlier period substituted for it. The people of the present day were also obliterated with the scenery, and we have the strange situation in which the village people who were around, as they must have been on that autumn day in 1957, were able to see the little group from HMS *Ganges* as they passed through the village, or squatted by the stream, but were themselves unobserved. In a letter written in 1988 Mr Laing said: 'Modern inhabitants must have seen us three sitting by the stream or wandering around.' They were, he said in a later letter, dressed in blue naval shirts, blue trousers, and boots.

There was thus some reason for Mr Laing's feeling that his group was being observed by unseen watchers while they were in the village. In some circumstances such feelings may take a more positive form. In her account of her second visit to the Petit Trianon in January 1902 Miss Jourdain said:

I was puzzling my way among the maze of paths in the wood when I heard a rustling behind me, which made me wonder why people in silk dresses came out on such a wet day; and I said to myself 'Just like French people'. I turned sharply to see who they were, but saw no one, and then, all in a moment, I had the same feeling as by the terrace in the summer, only in a much greater degree; it was as though I were closed in by a group of people who already filled the path, coming from behind and passing me. At one moment there seemed really no room for me. I heard some women's voices talking French, and caught the words 'Monsieur et Madame' said close to my ear. The crowd got scarce and drifted away.

(1955: 46)

It will be noted that although sounds were heard, and there was an overwhelming impression that people were in close proximity, no one was seen.

The feeling of eerieness described by Mr Laing was greatest by the stream, which, he remarked during our visit in 1990, now crossed the lane at an angle instead of straight across, as he remembered from 1957. I tried to clear up this point with the Highways Department of the Suffolk County Council. The Area Surveyor wrote in October 1990 that 'Over the years we have experienced many problems with potholes appearing in the ford and we were advised to use a concrete base. This was constructed approximately six years ago and to date has proved most successful although periodically we have to brush off the algae which forms on its surface and produces an extremely slippery covering to the ford.' It is clear from this that the stream could have followed a different course in 1957, if only by a yard or two, and this could result in difficulties of observation from a particular point. It was obvious to me during our visit that Mr Laing, standing on the southern side of the water-splash, had trouble in reconciling the view of buildings on the right-hand side of the street over the ford with what he remembered from 1957. This is understandable when the long period of time between the two visits is taken into consideration, and the Kersey he described in his letters from Australia is so different from the Kersey of today. I sent Mr Laing a picture, supplied by the Suffolk Record Office, of the water-splash and bridge as they were in 1930. He replied: 'the 1930 picture of the water-splash and bridge as they were in 1930 disturbs me. If I cover up the present ford and the cottage with the paling fence you have the big clear area I mention. Of course the background houses and church weren't there.'

He added: 'I also study and study the picture of the splash in 1930 a lot. There must have been something in Kersey in the past to leave such an impression. Just looking at it makes me feel gloomy and depressed.' As we will see from later case histories in this book, feelings of depression often accompany retrocognitive experiences, sometimes for no apparent reason, but it is not difficult to point to one devastating experience in the past that could have left an indelible impression on the village: the Black Death of 1349 in which, according to the church information sheet, a large proportion of the population died and the building of the church tower was put back by more than a century. It is possible that loss of population in the district led to the dissolution of the Augustinian priory, now a ruin near the northern end of the village, in 1444. It is not difficult to visualize how the little village, tucked into a fold in the fields, must have looked at the time of the Black Death and its aftermath with the empty cottages, the untended lane and fields, and the atmosphere of mourning everywhere.

Mr Laing is not alone in finding the village a depressing place. On my first visit to Bridge House, from which the butchery business was once conducted, Mrs Finch and Miss Gladys King said there was a deeply unhappy feeling in the village marked by the fact that there had been fourteen suicides there in the last sixty years – a large number in such a small place. Both took seriously the suggestion that the village might be haunted. At the Bell Inn the landlady, Mrs Lynne Coote, a Yorkshirewoman, declared that the inn was haunted. I found it rather difficult to ascertain what form the haunting took but apparently she saw what she described as 'skeleton faces'. A former landlord had hanged himself there. Members of the staff of the inn agreed that the village was a sad place. Obviously, not all members of the village community would share this impression. The Rev. Gerald Harrison, who was vicar of Kersey from 1981 to 1988, but did not live there, when asked for his impression of the village, replied: 'Kersey didn't come across to me as a "sad, haunted place". Like every village community it had its conflicts, some to do with absorbing the many incomers. But in retrospect I am much more aware of happinesses experienced there than sadnesses.'

In the final analysis, we rely on our opinion of the reliability of witnesses before we feel we can accept an account of an experience, particularly if it concerns happenings as strange as those in Versailles and Kersey, which have a certain number of features in common. In a letter to the *Journal* of the SPR for November 1953, Mr W. H. W. Sabine, who was critical of accounts of retrocognition in general, said: 'It has always been my view that the only ground on which the experience at the Petit Trianon recounted by Miss Moberly and Miss Jourdain could be dismissed is the ground of a calculated and consummately perpetuated fraud. Since the good faith of the narrators is universally admitted, I have never been able to understand how anyone could classify their experience as illusion – the misinterpretation of the normal surroundings.' I have given my reasons for not accepting the fraud hypothesis for the accounts of the happenings at Kersey and, just as Mr Sabine had confidence in the good faith of the authors of *An Adventure*, I have complete faith in my two correspondents in Australia. I received only one letter from Mr Crowley but it provided the necessary, indeed essential, confirmation of Mr Laing's account. Without it we would have had only one person's word for what took place, although there are circumstances in which information revealed by a single person's experience can be confirmed. It is, in a sense, disappointing that the third member of the party, Mr Baker, cannot confirm what took place. One of the interesting facts to emerge from the great Census of Hallucinations conducted by the SPR towards the end of the last century was that hallucinations tend to be forgotten with the passage of time, so perhaps it is not surprising that one member of a party of three could not remember what happened in Kersey more than thirty years earlier. The principal witness is, of course, Mr Laing, and favourable impression I formed of his reliability as a witness was confirmed by a personal meeting during an excursion to the scene of his experience in 1990.

One point still puzzled me. When Mr Laing and his companions entered the village in 1957 they saw before them a dusty, earthen track, such as there might have been in medieval times, but was there such a track at the time of their visit? I raised this point with the area surveyor, who replied: 'I would guess that Kersey Street was first surfaced using pea shingle and tar fairly soon after the Second World War. Prior to this time I would assume that The Street consisted of either dry bound Macadam or flints. Dry bound Macadam consists of stones of about 50 mm in diameter compacted using an infill of dust. I have no records to support this information and I cannot therefore guarantee that it is correct. However, the majority of roads in West Suffolk were surface dressed for the first time in the late 1940s.'

It appears that the youths from HMS *Ganges* could have trod not on an earthen track in 1957 but on a surfaced one. What their eyes told them could have been contradicted by the feel of their feet. When I pointed this out to Mr Laing after his return to Australia he replied that no real contradiction was involved. If the lane they trod in Kersey in 1957 was compared with a bush track in Australia the latter, though dusty in very dry weather, was still firm underfoot. There is an interesting field for further research here on the extent and limitation of hallucinatory experiences.

Cases of the quality of the Kersey experience of the three youths in 1957 very rarely see the light of day, possibly one or two times in a century, mainly because those involved do not understand the nature of the phenomena they have experienced and prefer to keep information about it to themselves, or to a small intimate circle, such as a family, in case they are thought 'odd' or fear for their sanity. I hope that one effect of this book will be to dispel such a fear.

Finally, Mr Laing is a Highlander and was probably more sensitive to the atmosphere than his companions although, as he stressed in his letters, they were all aware of the strangeness of what they were experiencing at the time. One of the most unusual features of Mr Laing's own experience (not mentioned by Crowley) was that in the village there was the fresh greenness of spring as compared with the hues of autumn in the trees and fields on the approach to Kersey. This alone is an indication of the mystical nature of the experience during which the curtain that hides the past was pulled aside and the landscape of an earlier age revealed.

It may be thought odd that it has taken more than thirty years for a story as strange as this to come to light. The reason, I feel, that this is so is that the person who has undergone an experience such as that described here has, as a rule, no means of assessing it and, lacking comprehension, he or she is inclined to dismiss it. In this first letter Mr Laing wrote: 'Perhaps you have other references to this [the experience he had described as having taken place at Kersey] in your archives.' He was not to know that such experiences with evidential features are very rare. A letter to the Society for Psychical Research (the address is given on p. 131) would have elicited a prompt reply. If only Mr Baker could have been interviewed at the time we would have had three witnesses to what took place in the village instead of two. Even so, we are fortunate that we have the testimony of the two witnesses to the extraordinary happenings on that Sunday morning in Kersey in 1957.

Chapter 2

Experience of a Vanished Street

A Nottinghamshire schoolboy out for a stroll in the city which he had known well all his life turned a corner 'and was suddenly struck with a feeling of having stepped into the past', he wrote to me in 1976 after reading my *Apparitions and Ghosts*. He found himself gazing into a cobbled street with old-fashioned cottages which seemed strangely out of place in a modern centre. Although he described the street to his mother and others, he was never able to find it again. Here is his story:

In the summer of 1961 I had just finished my 'O' level examinations [he was 16 at the time] and had a lot of time on my hands. One sunny afternoon I was strolling aimlessly round Nottingham, a city I knew extremely well, having lived there all my life. I was somewhere near the castle, but I was not sure exactly where, when I turned a corner and was suddenly struck with a feeling of having stepped into the past. I was looking into a narrow cobbled street on one side of which was a row of half-timbered cottages with shutters alongside the windows and window-boxes full of brightly coloured flowers – I seem to think they were mostly geraniums. There was no one in sight and the street was surprisingly quiet for somewhere near a city centre. It was obviously a cul-de-sac so I did not enter the street but turned round and carried on towards the castle, being surprised to find such a picturesque spot which I did not know. I later described it to my mother and other relatives, all of whom had lived in Nottingham all their lives, but none of them recognized the street from my description. Since then I have often looked for the street but without success and I decided the street no longer existed.

The sequel to this is that the Nottingham *Evening Post* ran a series of photographs of old Nottingham scenes, and I was interested to see, last year, a photo of the very street I had seen. The caption stated it to be Jessamine Cottages but I had a strange feeling when I read the street had been demolished in the mid-1950s. My mother spoke to Mr Dick Iliffe of the Nottingham Historical Film Unit (to whom the photo belonged) a few days later and he confirmed the date of the demolition. I suppose it is possible I had seen the street as a child but I do not consciously remember doing so and in any case I am sure of the year in which I saw it because of having just taken my exams.

My correspondent, Mr John Watson, is an engineer. His mother, Mrs Mary Watson, confirmed that she had been told about the experience at the time 'and when a picture of this very place appeared in the *Evening Post* he recognized it at once only to read that the property was demolished quite a time before John had seen it. It was most uncanny! The details in the picture were exact in every detail as John had described them to me.'

The City Secretary of Nottingham confirmed that Jessamine Cottages, off Castle Road, were demolished in 1956 and kindly enclosed a number of newspaper cuttings about them. He put me in touch with a member of the staff of the City Planning Office who used to live in one of the cottages. I wrote to this lady, Mrs Jessie Woodhouse, who explained that 'Jessamine Cottages were built above street level and were not accessible to vehicular traffic. Therefore, as the majority of the cottages were occupied by elderly people, most of the time the row of cottages would appear deserted.' She added that 'Castle Road, which ran below the level of the cottages, was a fairly busy road, although there would be quiet periods during the day'.

Jessamine Cottages, built in 1715, originally comprised the workhouse of St Nicholas, one of the three parishes of Nottingham at the time. In 1815 the workhouse was divided into tenements. Gradually they fell into disuse and many, in the 1950s, were overgrown with rambling weeds. In the 1940s there was much discussion, and lively controversy, in the press about how this picturesque corner of Nottingham might be preserved. The premises were offered by the corporation to Nottingham Archaeological Society at a nominal rent to serve as a possible headquarters and as repository of relics of bygone Nottingham, but this offer was refused because of the condition of the cottages and the cost involved in repairing them. When the time came to demolish the cottages they had been condemned for many years. Describing the cottages, a local writer said that 'Their picturesque gables, dormer windows and the patch of garden in front of them surrounded with hollyhocks, lupins and jessamine make an old-world atmosphere that never fails to enrapture visitors.' In 1956 they were demolished to make way for the People's College of Further Education, opened on 23 March 1961, which covers a considerably larger area than that occupied by the cottages. It was in the summer of 1961 that John Watson had his visionary experience of the cottages as they were in earlier years.

Mr Watson concedes that as a child he might have seen the cottages but he did not consciously remember doing so. A forgotten memory may have acted as the spur for his hallucinatory experience, but it does not follow that he had seen the cottages in the course of his childhood rambles. It is clear from material sent to me by the City Secretary that Jessamine Cottages were difficult of access. A paragraph in one of the local newspapers said that 'the cottages are built in the shape of three sides of a rectangle and stand on rock foundations high above neighbouring property, but they can be passed in Castle Road without notice'.

I raised a number of questions with Mr Watson about his experience and in a letter I received in 1977 he said:

Regarding Jessamine Cottages, I was sixteen at the time I 'saw' the street. I cannot remember having seen the street as a child although it is quite possible I may have walked in that area, possibly because it is close to Nottingham Castle, the grounds of which are a popular park. You ask about my description of the street as 'surprisingly quiet'. So far as I can remember after fifteen and a half years, the other street was quiet in the sense of there being little traffic, vehicular or pedestrian, but with the usual hum of city traffic in the air. The striking thing about Jessamine Cottages was not so much the fact that it was deserted but more the silence of it.

While discussing the incident with friends last week the question arose of what would have happened had I walked further into the street. Would I have passed temporarily into the past or would I have been likely to walk into any present-day obstruction without seeing it?

A somewhat similar question was asked by Mr Laing in his account of his experience in Kersey in the previous chapter. We will know the answer to such questions only when someone's curiosity compels him or her to carry out an experiment to test the reality of what is observed.

The silence Mr Watson noted during his experience accords with that which accompanied other experiences of a seemingly retrocognitive nature given in this book.

Chapter 3

Experience of
Vanished Buildings

Altandhu in Wester Ross in the Scottish Highlands is a little village
that was reasonably prosperous and busy a generation ago but is
now only sparsely populated. Visitors to this beautiful village are
few, except during the holiday season, because it is so far from the
beaten tourist track, but those that make their way there note the
remains of deserted croft houses, sometimes only a heap of ruins,
and what were once cultivated plots but are now no more than
poor grassland carrying a few sheep. The handful of crofters who
live there are mainly old people whose families have left home. In
summer the holiday visitors come, and among them is Mrs Gladys
McAvoy, then of Inverness, who wrote to me in 1971 about how
this remote spot had 'a wonderful peace and "other-worldliness"
that seems to change the nature of time'. It was certainly so for
her on 5 August 1966 when, during a walk, she 'saw' a house that
had been inhabited about two hundred years earlier but, so later
investigation proved, had vanished without trace. At the time Mrs
McAvoy was staying with her husband and family at the holiday
house that had been built for them seven years earlier.

At the other end of the village lives a crofter friend, a mile
distant, and it was to see her that I set out, with our dog, in
the morning of Friday, 5 August 1966. I remember feeling very
'vague' that day, a feeling I decided was the result of fatigue after
driving some 120 miles the day before, mainly along single-track
roads in the middle of the holiday season. I was pleasantly
relaxed too. The children – my daughter and her two cousins
– had been taken for a swim by my husband. I was enjoying
the walk on my own in the middle of a busy holiday. I passed
the ruin [of a croft] on my left and walked on fairly briskly, the

35

dog running ahead. I looked around, enjoying the view of the sea and islands to my left, and noticed the houses as I passed them. One I found particularly attractive. It lay immediately below the road, to my left, with the corner of the house abutting the road. Because it lay at an angle to the road I could see down into the 'garden' – just a grassy (or cobbled?) square as far as I remember. The house was of grey stone with the gable end nearest to the road and what struck me as of more interest than anything else was the fact that it had a chimney at both ends (as is usual in croft houses) and that *both* were smoking. I felt sure that it was a very busy house, though no one was about. With that thought I turned to look at our house to see if it looked 'busy' too – of course it didn't; we had no fire on and no one was about.

I continued my walk, still noticing my surroundings and wondered vaguely whose house I had just passed. I visited my friend but forgot to ask her. However, my husband called to collect me after a while and as we left I told him of the house I had noticed and asked him if he knew who lived there. He assured me that he had never seen it, but I insisted that I could point it out on the way home. We stopped at the place from which I had looked back at our house (I could 'pin-point' this as I had noticed how it stood in relation to the ruin), but there was, of course, nothing there – not even a heap of stones to suggest a house. However, I felt quite sure that there had, at one time, been such a house in that place and about a fortnight later while visiting our neighbours with my daughter (then aged 13) I told them of my experience and asked whether there had been a house there. They exchanged glances, then said, 'It will just mean that someone is thinking of building there.' We went on to talk of similar incidents that they remembered (such things are accepted by West Highlanders) until we all felt a little spooky. All this while a fifth member of the party, an old crofter who lived further along the village, stared at me but said nothing until he finally rose to go saying, 'I'll not go back by the hill tonight.'

Feeling a little dissatisfied by my neighbours' explanation I asked them again about the house I had seen. 'Yes,' they said at last. 'There was such a house just where you saw it. The corner was against the road because the house was built before the road and it was a busy house with a large family in it.' A daughter of that family, then over 90, still lived in the next village, Polbain, and I was told that the old crofter who sat and said nothing was her son-in-law. As such 'visions' are thought to be ill-omens I decided that their early reticence was on account of this (he did in fact die very soon afterwards, but not the old lady, who was not told). However, a justification for their 'interpretation' came a few months later. The local postman/crofter, also from Altandhu, was a daily visitor to my neighbours' house. He was going to be married and spoke of plans to restore a nearby ruin. However, they told me, he one day announced quite unexpectedly that he had given up that idea and was thinking of building a bungalow – on the site of 'my' house. They had said nothing to him about my experience, but was their knowledge of it passed on to him telepathically and so influenced his thoughts? Or did he think of building the bungalow *before* I had my vision and did I pick up the 'message' at the moment I passed the site and then did my mind 'slip back in time' and so see the former house? Whatever its origins,the experience is still very vivid in my memory.

Mrs McAvoy's husband added a note confirming his wife's account. He said: 'I confirm that on our short drive home (only about a mile) on 5 August 1966 my wife asked me who lived in the house she had seen. I assured her of its non-existence and she pointed out to me where she had "seen" it, about an hour previously.'

Mrs McAvoy's crofter friends, Duncan and Mary MacLean, told her that the house she had 'seen' in her vision was occupied nearly two hundred years ago by a Mr MacLean and his wife, born Kirsty Stewart. They had had four children who were adults when Duncan and Mary were born (both of them died in their eighties). The house was a ruin in Duncan and Mary's childhood. They said it was very familiar to them as they passed it on their way to and from school. They remembered that the fireplace and part of the chimney were then intact. They confirmed that there was an enclosed area outside the house and on the seaward side. They remembered this as the family continued to cultivate this patch after they moved to a larger house. Mrs McAvoy said that this 'seems to correspond to the walled enclosure or "garden" into which I looked'.

I asked Mrs McAvoy how long her experience of the house had lasted. She said:

It is very difficult to say how long the 'house' was in sight. I was walking at a moderate speed and as far as I remember I was quite suddenly aware that it was there, to my left, a little in front of me and that I could see the gable wall near the road. . . . I looked long enough to note that no one was about, though I had a clear mental picture of *something* [underlined] in that enclosure and that the chimneys were smoking. All this might have taken no more than a minute. I can't say for sure that it was still there after I had turned to look at our house, but surely I would have noticed if it had vanished. . . . One other incident has always puzzled me. After walking on for some distance, still feeling, as I said, a little 'vague', I noticed a garden full of flowers to my right. This house is well known to me and I probably took little notice of it at the time. I do remember, however, a small flower-filled enclosure beside the road, with a little gate and path and behind it the garden wall proper with flowers growing above and near it. I told Mary MacLean about this and she confirmed that it used to be a lovely garden, but I have never seen it even remotely like this since. The owner seldom lives in it [the house] and it is used mainly for short holiday lets and looks very unkempt by now. However, a few flowers do appear over the wall occasionally though I have never seen the little flower-filled enclosure in front again.

It is apparent from this that Mrs McAvoy's state of hallucination continued after she had seen the house.

The next case also comes from Scotland. In 1953 Ms Nan Dodd was an usherette in the Caley Cinema in Lothian Road, Edinburgh, when, to her surprise, she saw a couple sitting at a table in what was know to *habitués* of the cinema as the 'jury box'. The woman was pouring tea from a silver teapot for the man. Just then the house telephone rang, and Ms Dodd answered it, but there was no sign of the pair when she glanced again in their direction. 'The glimpse must have lasted for one or two seconds', she wrote to me.

Her niece, Mrs Meredith, who drew the case to my attention (Chapter 6), said that Ms Dodd was 'very sensitive psychically and has had many similar experiences'. Mrs Meredith wrote: 'I believe that one of the testing grounds for psychic experiences are that they are impossible to forget and this particular incident (likewise) was never forgotten.' However, it was not until 1986 that a possible explanation was forthcoming. When the Caley's days as a cinema were over (it is now a discothèque), a local newspaper, the *Tollcross Times*, published an account of the building's history. It had once been an hotel. The couple whom Ms Dodd had 'seen' were presumably guests at the hotel.

'As far as I know,' said Mrs Meredith, 'Nan never mentioned this incident to anyone for fear of being thought "crazy", so unfortunately there is no one who could verify it. In fact, she never told me about it until after she had read the newspaper article and I can recall that the excitement in her accompanying letter was quite electric.'

Mrs Meredith explained that the 'jury box' was an enclosed area situated behind the balcony seats barrier and the main entrance aisleway. 'It looked very grand, like a private box in a theatre, and this made many patrons reluctant to sit in it, believing that it must be reserved for VIPs. It was an interesting place with a very good feeling about it (positive energy, I suppose).'

The article from the *Tollcross Times* is headed 'FROM THE ASHES OF A ZEPPELIN BOMB THE CALEY PALACE'. It goes on to describe a Zeppelin raid on the night of 2 April 1916. Among the buildings hit was the County Hotel in Lothian Road. A bomb ripped through the roof and upper storeys, causing considerable damage to adjoining buildings.

It was from the ashes of this disaster that the Caley Palais was to emerge six years later when the Caley Picture House Company took over the site. Within eight months they had cleared away the remains of the County Hotel and built a stylish new cinema.

Over the years the Caley became a much loved venue for filmgoers, and its name was to be heard mispronounced on countless visitors' lips. But the pressures of the television age did not leave the Caley unscathed and in 1986 it closed. After 63 years as a cinema the Caley has finally be transformed into a discothèque [known as the Century 2000 disco].

From an evidential point of view it is unfortunate that Ms Dodd's experience was not told to anyone before she found out that the cinema had once been an hotel, but her reticence is understandable.

Chapter 4

The 'Adventure' at Versailles

When Miss Annie Moberly and Miss Eleanor Jourdain went for a walk in the park of the Petit Trianon at Versailles on 10 August 1901, a Saturday, they had an 'adventure', described in a book with that title (*An Adventure*), which, when published ten years later, created a sensation and aroused controversy that has continued to the present day. The story the two ladies told was so astounding that it is not surprising that the publishers, Macmillan, felt it necessary to insert a note that 'the ladies whose adventure is described in these pages have for various reasons preferred not to disclose their real names, but the signature appended to the Preface are the only fictitious words in the book. The Publishers guarantee that the Authors have put down what happened to them as faithfully and accurately as was in their power.' The signature to the Preface are those of Elizabeth Morrison (Miss Moberly) and Frances Lamont (Miss Jourdain).

The book was an immediate success. The first edition was published in January 1911; it was twice reprinted in February, reprinted again in March, April and July, and reprinted once in 1912. Because of the continuing demand for the book a second edition, with appendix and maps, was published in 1913. This edition is now scarce. Third and fourth editions followed. The fifth edition, which was the last English edition to be authorized by the owner of the copyright, the late Dame Joan Evans, was in 1955. She had decided not to allow the book to be reprinted because she considered there was a natural explanation for what the two ladies said they saw, but this view was rejected by others for reasons which I will give later. However, Dr Evans relented to allow an edition of the book to be published in French, and in 1988 Dr Michael H. Coleman, a member of the SPR, published *The Ghosts of the*

Trianon, subtitled 'The Complete Adventure', with the ladies' two accounts given in full and accounts of other investigations into the case. Dr Coleman states that 'with the various reprints of the five successive editions, there have been some twenty impressions of the book since its first appearance in 1991'. The extraordinary appeal of the book is due in part, I feel, to the identification of a figure seen by one of the two ladies, Miss Moberly, with the tragic Queen Marie Antoinette. The identity of the two ladies was revealed in the fourth edition of the book, published by Faber in 1931. A possible reason for their reticence was that Miss Moberly, the daughter of a Bishop of Salisbury, was the first principal of St Hugh's Hall (later College), Oxford, in which post she was succeeded by Miss Jourdain, the daughter of a Derbyshire vicar.

The two women first visited the palace of Versailles, and, as there was time to spare, decided to walk through the grounds to the two Trianons. 'By not asking the way we went an unnecessarily long way round – by the great flight of steps from the fountains and down the central avenue as far as the head of the long pond', said Miss Moberly. 'The weather had been very hot all the week, but on this day the sky was a little overcast and the sun shaded. There was a lively wind blowing, the woods were looking their best, and we both felt particularly vigorous. It was a most enjoyable walk.' After reaching the beginning of the long water they struck away to the right down a woodland glade until they came obliquely to the other water, close to a building which they rightly concluded to be the Grand Trianon. They passed it on their left hand and came up a broad green drive perfectly deserted. If they had followed it they would have come immediately to the Petit Trianon, but not knowing the way they crossed the drive and went up a lane in front of them. Miss Moberly was surprised that Miss Jourdain did not ask the way from a woman who was shaking a white cloth out of the window of a building at the corner of the lane, but followed, supposing that she knew where she was going. Talking about England and mutual acquaintances there, they went up the lane and made a sharp turn to the right past some buildings. They looked in at an open doorway and saw the end of a carved staircase, but as no one was about they did not like to go in.

There were three paths in front of them, and as they saw two men a little ahead on the centre one they followed it and asked them the way. Afterwards they spoke of them as gardeners, but, according to Miss Moberly, 'they were really very dignified officials, dressed in long greyish-green coats with small three-cornered hats'. Miss Jourdain, who was the questioner, said: 'They told us, in answer to my enquiry, to go straight on. I remember repeating my question, because they answered in a seemingly casual and mechanical way, but only got the same answer, in the same manner.' As they were standing there she saw to the right of them a detached, solidly built cottage, with stone steps at the door. A woman and a girl were standing at the doorway, and she particularly noticed their unusual dress; each wore a white kerchief tucked into her bodice, and the girl's dress, though she looked only 13 or 14, was down to her ankles.

The two women walked briskly forward, talking as before, but, said Miss Moberly,

> from the moment we left the lane an extraordinary depression had come over me, which, in spite of every effort to shake off, steadily deepened. I was anxious that my companion should not discover the sudden gloom upon my spirits, which became quite overpowering on reaching the point where the path ended, being crossed by another, right and left. In front of us was a wood, within which, and overshadowed by trees, was a light garden kiosk, circular, and like a small bandstand, by which a man was sitting. There was no green sward, but the ground was covered with rough grass and dead leaves as in a wood. the place was so shut in that we could not see beyond it. Everything suddenly looked unnatural, therefore unpleasant; even the trees behind the building seemed to have become flat and lifeless, *like a wood worked in tapestry*. There were no effects of light and shade. It was all intensely still.

Miss Jourdain, describing that part of the walk, said:

> there· was a feeling of depression and lonelinesss about the place. I began to feel as if I was walking in my sleep; the heavy dreaminess was oppressive. At last we came upon a path crossing ours, and saw in front of us a building consisting of some columns roofed in, and set back in the trees. Seated on the steps was a man with a heavy black cloak round his shoulders, and wearing a slouch hat. At that moment the eerie feeling which

had begun in the garden culminated in a definite impression of something uncanny and fear-inspiring. The man slowly turned his face, which was marked by smallpox: his complexion was very dark. The expression was very evil and yet unseeing, and though I did not feel that he was looking particularly at us, I felt a repugnance to going past him.

In order to avoid the evil-looking man in the slouch hat, the two ladies decided to go to the right. It was a great relief at that moment to hear someone running up to them in breathless haste. Connecting the sound with the gardeners – the two men in long greyish-green coats – Miss Moberly turned and ascertained that there was no-one on the paths, either to the side or behind; but at almost the same moment she suddenly perceived another man quite close to them, who had, apparently, just come over, round, or through, a rock that shut out the view at the junction of the paths. The suddenness of his appearance was something of a shock. Miss Moberly considered that the newcomer was 'distinctly a gentleman'. He was tall, with large dark eyes, and had crisp, curling black hair under a sombrero hat. He was handsome, and the effect of the hair was to make him look like an old picture. He looked greatly excited as he called out to them, 'Mesdames, Mesdames, il ne faut [pronounced *fout*] pas passer par là.' He then waved his arm, and said with great animation, 'Par ici . . . cherchez la maison.' Miss Moberly was so surprised at this eagerness that she looked up at him again, and to this he responded with a little backward movement and what she considered to be a most peculiar smile. Though she could not follow all he said, it was clear that he was determined that they should go to the right and not to the left. As this fell in with her own wish she went instantly towards a little bridge on the right, and turning her head to join Miss Jourdain in thanking him found, to her surprise, that he was not there, but the running began again and from the sound it was close behind them.

Silently the two ladies passed over the small rustic bridge which crossed a tiny ravine. Beyond the little bridge their pathway led under trees; it skirted a narrow meadow of long grass, bounded on the further side by trees, and very much overshadowed by trees growing in it. This gave the whole place a sombre look suggestive of dampness, and shut out the view of the house they were seeking until they were close to it. The house was a square, solidly built, small country-house – quite different from what Miss Moberly expected. The long windows looking north into the English garden, where they stood, were shuttered. There was a terrace round the north and west sides of the house, and on the rough grass, which grew quite up to the terrace, and with her back to it, a woman was sitting, holding out a paper as though to look at it at arm's length.

Miss Moberly supposed her to be sketching and to have brought her own camp stool:

> It seemed as though she must be making a study of trees [Miss Moberly wrote] for they grew close in front of her, and there seemed nothing else to sketch. She saw us, and when we passed close by on her left hand [side] she turned and looked full at us. It was not a young face and (though rather pretty) it did not attract me. She had on a shady white hat perched on a good deal of fair hair that fluffed round her forehead. Her light summer dress was arranged on her shoulders in handkerchief fashion, and there was a little line of either green or gold near the edge of the handkerchief, which showed me that it was *over*, not tucked into her bodice, which was cut low, her dress was long-waisted, with a good deal of fullness in the skirt, which seemed to be short. I thought she was a tourist, but that her dress was old-fashioned and rather unusual (though people were wearing fichu bodices that summer). I looked straight at her; but some indescribable feeling made me turn away, annoyed at her being there.
>
> (1931: 48)

This description is important because the 'sketching lady' was later assumed to have been the apparition of Queen Marie Antoinette. It later transpired, to Miss Moberly's astonishment, that Miss Jourdain had not seen this figure.

The two ladies went up the steps on to the terrace, but Miss Moberly was 'beginning to feel as though we were walking in a dream – the stillness and oppressiveness were so unnatural. Again I saw the lady, this time from behind, and noticed that her fichu was pale green.' They crossed the terrace to the south-west corner and looked over into the *cour d'honneur*; and then turned back, and seeing that one of the long windows overlooking the French garden was unshuttered they were going towards it when they were interrupted. The terrace was prolonged at right angles in front of what seemed to be a second house.

The door of it suddenly opened, and a young man stepped out on to the terrace, banging the door behind him. He had the jaunty manner of a footman, but no livery, and called to us, saying that the way into the house was by the *cour d'honneur*, and offered to show us the way round. He looked inquisitively amused as he walked by us down the French garden till we came to an entrance into the front drive. We came out sufficiently near the front lane we had been in to make me wonder why the garden officials had not directed us back instead of telling us to go forward. When we were at the front entrance we were kept waiting for the arrival of a merry French wedding party.

(1931: 49)

Miss Jourdain said that the 'feeling of dreariness' was very strong as they passed through the French garden and it continued until they actually reached the front entrance to the Petit Trianon and looked round the rooms in the wake of the French wedding party.

By this time the two ladies 'felt quite lively again', according to Miss Moberly. Coming out of the *cour d'honneur* they took a little carriage that was standing there and drove back to the Hotel des Réservoirs in Versailles, where they had tea, but neither of them was inclined to talk, and did not mention any of the events of the afternoon. After tea they walked back to the station.

For a whole week the two ladies did not allude to the happenings of that afternoon. When Miss Moberly began writing a letter about their expeditions during the week and 'the scenes came back one by one', she said that 'the same sensation of dreamy unnatural oppression came over me so strikingly' that she asked her companion: 'Do you think that the Petit Trianon is haunted?' Miss Jourdain's reply was a prompt 'Yes I do'.

I estimate that the walk through the park would take the two ladies about thirty minutes.

On 2 January 1902 Miss Jourdain paid a second visit to Versailles. It was a cold and wet day. She did not retrace the old route but went along a path leading to the Hameau, a little village in the park where Marie Antoinette and ladies of the court had played at being dairymaids. There had been none of the eerie feeling she had experienced with her friend the previous August 'but on crossing a bridge to go to the Hameau the old feeling returned in full force; it was as if I had crossed a line and was suddenly in a circle of influence'. To the left she saw a tract of park-like ground, the trees bare and very scanty. She noticed a cart being filled with sticks by two labourers who wore tunics and capes with pointed hoods, one a sort of terra-cotta red and the other deep blue. She turned aside for an instant – not more – to look at the Hameau, and when she looked back again 'men and cart were completely out of sight, and this surprised me, as I could see a long way in every direction'. Miss Jourdain then went on to the Hameau. The houses were all built near a sheet of water, 'and the old oppressive feeling of the last year was noticeable, especially under the balcony of the Maison de la Reine, and near a window in what I afterwards found to be the Laiterie. I really felt a great reluctance to go near the window to look in, and when I did so I found it shuttered inside.' When walking along a path in a belt of trees near the Hameau, Miss Jourdain heard a rustling behind her which made her wonder why people in silk dresses came out on such a wet day. She turned sharply to see who they were, but saw no one, 'and then, all in a moment, I had the same feeling as by the terrace in the summer, only in a much greater degree; it was as though I were closed in by a group of people who already filled the path, coming from behind and passing me. The crowd got scarce and drifted away, and then faint music as of a band, not far off, was audible.' It later transpired that a band had not played in the park that day.

Miss Moberly paid her second visit to the Trianon on Monday, 4 July 1904, being accompanied by Miss Jourdain and a Frenchwoman who had not heard their story. On Saturday of the same week they went again, this time unaccompanied. Both days were brilliant and hot. The dust and glare, the trams, and the comers and goers were entirely different from the 'quietness and solitude' of their visit in 1901. They also found the scenery greatly changed. Miss Moberly said:

> To add to the impossibility of recalling our first visit, in every corner we came across groups of noisy merry people walking or sitting in the shade. Garden seats placed everywhere, and stalls for fruit and lemonade took away from any idea of desolation. The commonplace unhistorical atmosphere was totally inconsistent with the air of silent mystery by which we had been so much oppressed . . . I had not expected such complete disillusionment.
>
> (1955: 51)

Miss Moberly and Miss Jourdain later gave answers to questions they had been asked after the first edition appeared. They said that when they met three months after the first visit to the park they talked it over and found that Miss Jourdain had not seen the 'sketching lady' and that Miss Moberly had not seen the cottage, or the woman and girl in its doorway. This made them decide to write separate accounts of their visit in order to find the discrepancies but with no idea of making exhaustive histories. Miss Jourdain, in her story, used the words 'uncanny' and 'eerie' to describe her feelings, but they did not mean that she had the least idea at the time that any of the people encountered was unreal or ghostly; this was still more true of the scenery.

Their answer to the suggestion that they were in a state of 'suspended consciousness' during the walk was:

> Our conversation and sense of the quiet continuity of things remained unbroken, and, in spite of oppression, we believed ourselves to be particularly wide awake and on the alert. When we were first asked whether the man from the side building was real or not we laughed at the idea of any unreality; it was all so quietly natural that we are still uncertain whether the tall gardener belonged to another century or not [the reference here is apparently to a gardener who had given directions to Miss Jourdain on her second visit in January 1902]. It has taken us nine years to work out all the details which bear witness to the strangeness of what we saw and did and to justify us in our present conviction that from the moment of our leaving the lane until we emerged into the avenue we were on enchanted ground.

It had been suggested to the two ladies that their story could be explained by people posing for a film but they dismissed this:

> No amount of masqueraders explains to us the ease with which we dismissed from sight and hearing the usual August crowds in the middle of a fine afternoon, and the impossibility of harmonizing our recollections of the scenery with anything but the old maps and records . . . . Even should it be proved that a cinematograph had been taken that very day, it would not be a possible explanation to us. The groups we saw were small

47

and isolated from one another. There was the deepest silence everywhere and no sunshine; whilst the light was the worst possible for a picture, for the sky was overcast. And, though whilst we stood there an indefinable air of strangeness dropped over everything, including the tall forest trees, it was not of a kind that could be accounted for by fictitious scenery. The people moved and spoke as usual, but their words were extraordinarily difficult to catch.

(1955: 95)

Publication of *An Adventure* brought to light accounts of earlier experiences in the park at Versailles. The fourth edition of the book in 1931 contained an addition: an appendix (dropped from the fifth edition in 1955), which told of the meeting of Mr and Mrs John Crooke and their son Stephen Crooke with the two authors in 1914. The Crooke family, who were English, lived in a flat in the rue Maurepas at Versailles in 1907 and 1908. In 1908, three years before *An Adventure* was published, they had – all three persons together – twice seen the 'sketching lady'. Both times it had been in July and at the Grand Trianon. The first time she was sitting in the garden, close to the glass colonnade, on a low stool on a green bank where, in fact, there was no green bank, but only gravel and flower-beds. The second time she was sitting below the balustrade, over which one can look from the Grand Trianon to the canal below. On both occasions she was dressed in a light, cream-coloured skirt, white fichu, and a white, untrimmed, flopping hat. The skirt was full and much gathered, and the lady spread it round her. both times she appeared to be sketching. 'They never doubted that she was ghostly because of the peculiar way in which she appeared and disappeared, "seeming to grow out of, and to retire into, the scenery with a little quiver of adjustment"'. Her hair was fair. The Crooke family were artists; they had carefully noted the lady and had observed that, though she seemed quite real, all the contours of her figure and her general bearing were not what they were accustomed to then. 'Not only her dress, but she herself, belonged to another century.'
On one occasion Mrs Crooke had met a man in eighteenth-century costume with the small three-cornered hat as described by the two authors. Mr and Mrs Crooke had seen a woman in the grounds in an old-fashioned dress picking up sticks. They had

noticed the flattened appearance of the trees. One day, when he was alone, Mr Crooke had heard music coming over the water from the Belvédère, where certainly none was being performed. It was a stringed band playing old music, and he enjoyed listening to it for nearly a quarter of an hour.

The Crooke family mentioned a curious hissing sound that sometimes came when things were about to appear, possibly suggesting some electrical condition, and they also spoke of the vibration in the air which sometimes accompanied vision. On hearing this in 1914, Miss Moberly and Miss Jourdain immediately looked in the Almanack and found that 10 August 1901, the day of their 'adventure', had been remarkable for an electrical storm all over Europe.

The *Occult Review* of 1912 contained an account of a visit by a man and his wife to the Petit Trianon about a year before *An Adventure* was published. They came in at one of the gates and walked through what appeared to them to be a wood, at the end of which was a little hamlet of small houses. As they came round the corner the wife saw a woman leaning out of the window of one of the houses shaking out what appeared to be a large sheet or table-cloth. She remarked: 'Why, I had no idea people still lived in these houses here', whereupon her husband, who had not seen the figure, replied: 'Of course no one lives in them. Don't be so silly! I expect they are all locked up, and you couldn't get in even if you wanted to.' After *An Adventure* appeared they were so struck by it that they returned to the Trianon, and to their surprise neither of them recognized a single thing. They found no trace whatever of either the trees or the houses they had noticed on the previous occasion. instead of the thick wood they had traversed there was only a broad path, and where the little houses had been there was no sign of any dwellings whatever. The wife, on reading *An Adventure*, 'recalled having seen both the ploughman and the gardeners mentioned in that work; but had not at that time called her husband's attention to them, thinking they were merely ordinary labourers whose presence there was an everyday occurrence; but she had remarked on the woman who was shaking the linen out of the window and they had both noticed the row of houses and the trees [in fact, Miss Jourdain had mentioned seeing a plough, not a ploughman].'

The informant in this case was the Hon. Mrs Greville Nugent, who knew the people concerned. They were, according to Mr Colin Smythe, the publisher, Robert Gregory, son of the well-known Irish writer Lady Gregory, and his wife Margaret. I am grateful to Sir Patrick Macrory for sending me this information.

Accounts of other 'adventures' in the park gradually emerged. One concerned a visit by Miss Clare M. Burrow, at the time a mistress in a school for girls at Haslemere, Surrey, and a former pupil, Miss Anne Lambert, later Lady Hay, in early October, 1928. Miss Burrow said that, after exploring the great palace at Versailles, they visited the Grand Trianon and found themselves 'practically alone' when they turned into the long, green, statued avenue which they hoped would lead them to the Petit Trianon. They soon came upon a deserted building hemmed in by nettles and a strange feeling of depression came over her; they ceased to talk and hurried on until the ruined Hameau came into sight and from the window of a farmhouse near the lake a woman looked down on them. On turning to look for the Temple of Love among the trees they saw an old man whom they judged to be an official, as he was clad in an old green and silver uniform, approaching down a side avenue. Miss Burrow called to him, seeking information about the elusive Trianon; he replied by shouting sentence after sentence in hoarse and unintelligible French, as if in great haste. Something sinister in his face caused them to hurry on, and looking back they saw that he had completely vanished. The feeling of depression increased and it was with relief that they saw the Petit Trianon among the trees.

Miss Lambert also experienced the feeling of depression. She did not see the woman at the window but certainly saw the man in the out-of-date costume at a point soon after they had entered the garden, and distinctly recollected the sound of his voice, as he seemed to be talking in some strange language or patois. Both women were sure they had not heard of Miss Moberly's and Miss Jourdain's 'adventure' before they went to Versailles.

A French member of the SPR, Monsieur M. Dayet, got in touch with Miss Burrow and as a result was able to correct two errors in her account. The reference to the Hameau should be to the farm buildings near the Gardeners' Gate, and the reference to the Temple of Love should be to the Belvédère. With the aid of a map M. Dayet worked out with Miss Burrow the route she and her companion took, and it was clear that the man in green was encountered quite soon after they had entered the garden near the Belvédère.

Another 'adventure' concerned a London solicitor and his wife who visited the grounds of the Trianons on 21 May 1955. There was an extraordinary feeling of tenseness in the air; the weather was very close and oppressive after a heavy thunderstorm. The solicitor's wife felt 'unaccountably depressed'. They had seen no one since leaving the Grand Trianon to pass through the grounds of the Petit Trianon on the way to Marie Antoinette's village. Suddenly the sun came out and they saw, coming down a long grassy avenue on the right, which joined their path ahead, a woman between two men. The woman's dress was yellow of an unusual brilliance. The men wore long coats, open in front and nearly down to their knees at the back. they had black breeches, black stockings, black shoes with silver buckles and black hats. The solicitor felt no surprise when he saw these figures. Suddenly he became aware the the little group approaching them had vanished. 'That's odd,' he said to his wife, 'where have those persons gone?' The solicitor's wife, in her account of the disappearance, said: 'Then a peculiar thing happened. It was as though a curtain were drawn across my mind, obliterating the vision, and I entirely forgot them till we reached the spot where I had seen them, when my husband said: "That's odd. Did you see a lady with two gentlemen walking towards us? What's happened to them? They've vanished,"' The solicitor's wife had indeed seen the three figures and particularly admired the colour of the woman's dress. Her husband had read *An Adventure* the previous year.

Mr Jack Wilkinson, a poultry farmer, of Levens, near Kendal, Westmorland, his wife, Mrs Clara Wilkinson, and their 4-year-old son had an 'adventure' on 10 October 1949 when they visited the park at Versailles. It was a fine sunny day. They entered the park by the statue of Neptune and approached the Grand Trianon by way of the cottages and garden nurseries. As they came out of the woods at 11 a.m. they saw a woman standing on top of the steps of the Trianon about 50 yards away. What impressed them immediately was her costume. She was wearing a light gold-coloured crinoline-type dress reaching to the ground, had on a large picture hat, and was carrying a stick or parasol. She was of medium height, with dark ringlets to her shoulders, and, according to Mrs Wilkinson, was aged between 25 and 30. There was nothing ghostlike about her. All three saw the figure. Mr and Mrs Wilkinson felt astonished at seeing someone like that in the park. As they walked towards the

51

building the woman moved to the balustrade overlooking the arm of the grand canal. Not wishing to watch her all the time, they turned their attention to the building, and when they looked in her direction after a few minutes she had disappeared. They went at once to the balustrade, feeling 'a bit queer', in Mr Wilkinson's words, but could see no sign of the figure, which had been in view for two or three minutes. The Wilkinsons had not seen anyone else since entering the park. In reply to a question about his mood, Mr Wilkinson said, 'We cannot remember being in any special mood, except there was a noticeable quiet and stillness about the place.' He had not, he said, read *An Adventure*.

Another strange experience was that of Mrs Elizabeth Hatton, formerly of Oxford, who, early in September 1938, was walking down an avenue in the park of the Petit Trianon towards Marie Antoinette's village when suddenly, about 6 feet from her, two figures appeared. They were dressed as peasants and were drawing along a little wooden trundle cart with logs of wood on it. They passed close by without saying a word. Mrs Hatton said: 'I was completely baffled and turned to watch where they were going . . . as I watched them they seemed gradually to vanish.' The time was about midday, the sun was shining, and Mrs Hatton was alone. I asked Mrs Hatton if she had read *An Adventure*, or heard the Versailles case discussed *before* she had her experience, and she replied that she had not.

Miss Moberly and Miss Jourdain spent nearly ten years carrying out research before publishing the results. Miss Moberly considered that there was a likeness between the features of the woman she had seen sketching and those in a portrait of the queen (Marie Antoinette) by Wertmüller and, with her friend, came to the conclusion that the figures they had seen in the park could have been there in 1789, the last year in which Marie Antoinette visited the park before the Revolution. All their research centred round this date and the results were not convincing.

Some harsh criticism followed publication of the book. Mrs Henry Sidgwick, a woman of outstanding intellectual ability, considered, in a review of *An Adventure* in the *Proceedings* of the SPR in 1911, that 'it does not seem to use that, on the evidence before us, there is sufficient ground for supposing anything supernormal to have occurred at all. The persons and things seen were, we should judge, the real persons and things the seers supposed them to be at the time, probably decked out by tricks of memory (and after the idea of haunting had occurred to them), with some additional details of costume suitable to the time of Marie Antionette.'

Some of the most harsh criticism came from Mr J. R. Sturge-Whiting in his book *The Mystery of Versailles*, subtitled *A Complete Solution* (1937), with an approving introduction by Harry Price. Sturge-Whiting considered that the whole experience could be explained in natural terms, mainly because the two ladies had become confused about the location of features of the park. In my opinion Mr Sturge-Whiting seems to have missed the point that a vital clue to the two ladies' experiences in the park is offered by their state of mind at the time. Referring to Miss Jourdain's visits to the Trianon he said that 'on two or three subsequent occasions she experienced a recurrence of the old strange condition . . . to my mind they form the weakest link in the remarkable chain, and in the best interests of the story should have been left out altogether'. He considered that the experiences of the Crooke family in 1908 when they all saw the 'sketching lady' were 'little more than a sidelight on the peculiar mentality of its members', and that their account should not have been included in the fourth edition. This, in my view, is selective reporting indeed.

In *The Ghosts of Versailles* (1957) Mrs Lucille Iremonger took a cool and critical look at the Versailles 'adventure' but retained an open mind. In the latest assessment of the case Dr Michael H. Coleman in his book *The Ghosts of the Trianon* (1988) is, in general, dismissive, and concludes that 'the time now seems appropriate, fifty years after the death of their surviving author [Miss Moberly], to relegate the Ghosts of the Trianon to the limbo of those fictional ghosts which so thrilled our Victorian and Edwardian ancestors but which carry little conviction today'.

An additional point of criticism to those outlined above was that the figures seen by the two ladies could have been those of Count Robert de Montesquiou, a noted man of fashion who owned a house in Versailles, and his friends who staged historical tableaux in the park in which one of the women dressed as Marie Antionette. It was this argument that seemed particularly convincing to Dame Joan Evans, a friend of the authors and inheritor of the copyright of the book (she had written the introduction to the fifth edition of *An Adventure* in 1955), so much so that she decided not to authorize any more English editions. However, Dr Evans seems to have overlooked the fact that Count Robert was no longer living in Versailles at the time of the visit of the two ladies and, even more important, that people of fashion made a point of leaving Paris in August, so it was most unlikely that the count and his friends would have been there at that time of the year.

Despite the criticisms listed above, the interest of readers in the 'adventure' remained unabated and the voices of others who took a different view of the experiences of Miss Moberly and Miss Jourdain began to be heard. One influential commentator was Mr G. W. Lambert, a respected former president of the SPR. Others were O. A. and M. E. Gibbons, husband and wife, who compiled a symposium on *The Trianon Adventure* (1958). They, like Guy Lambert, carried out intensive research, which included scrutiny of the national archives and repeated visits to the park of the Petit Trianon. What was important was that they had an open mind about the date to which the 'adventure' could apply, and, unlike Miss Moberly and Miss Jourdain, were not obsessed with the events of 1789.

The Petit Trianon was intended by King Louis XV to be the home of his mistress, the Marquise de Pompadour, but she died before it was completed, and her successor, Madame du Barry, occasionally lived in the mansion when it was taken over by the King on 9 September 1770. The King, who took a great interest in the park and gardens, died in May 1774. The new King, Louis XVI, gave the Petit Trianon and its grounds to his queen, Marie Antionette, who immediately planned big changes to the park; these were carried out in 1776. Research revealed that a tall rock had once stood in the place where the two ladies said they had seen it and that the park had once contained a circular pavilion (Miss Moberly did a sketch of it from memory). The Petit Trianon originally had a large kitchen block but this was demolished so that a chapel could be built; this was finished in 1773. King Louis XV had a small menagerie and home farm in the grounds and a plan by Gabriel, the royal architect, shows a carriageway leading to the Allée de la Menagerie, as the broad way out was called. The southern end of this route had been obliterated by 1771 at the latest. The young man who stepped from a door in the mansion to direct the two ladies 'had the jaunty air of a footman', according to Miss Moberly, which would not be surprising if he had come from a kitchen, not a chapel. There are two doors, only a few feet apart, out of which the young man could have emerged, and there is some doubt as to which one it was. In the course of their subsequent inquiries both ladies were to discover that both sets of doors had been locked for many years and that the floorings within were alike broken and unusable.

Attempts by Mr Lambert and Mr and Mrs Gibbons to identify the figures seen in the park were unsuccessful except for the two men in green uniforms who could have been the royal gardeners, Claude Richard, who in 1770 was 65, and his son Antoine, then aged 35. They lived in houses near the Gardeners' Gate by which the two ladies had entered the park. It is known that up to 1775 or 1776 the Richards, father and son wore green because a document in the national archives setting out Queen Marie Antoinette's wishes for her Petit Trianon includes the phrase: 'It is thought that as the Richards are in green they ought to be in red with blue velvet facings.' This had the King's agreement.

Mr Lambert considered that, taking only the visit of 10 August 1901 into account, eight features could be listed which were quite inconsistent with the 1901 scene; they formed 40 per cent of the twenty distinguishable features listed in the two separate narratives of Miss Moberly and Miss Jourdain, a much higher proportion than one would expect to find in the circumstances. He could have added a ninth feature. By probing with a kitchen poker in the soft loamy soil Mr and Mrs Gibbons found the foundation of the walls of a cottage on the spot where Miss Jourdain saw a woman and a girl. Mr Lambert believed that the two ladies may have seen the park as it was in August 1770, just before the King took over the house. At this time Marie Antoinette had been married to the Dauphin for only a few months and was not yet 15. This disposes of Miss Moberly's suggestion that the 'sketching lady' she saw was the apparition of the ill-fated queen.

It seems to me that critics of the 'adventure' have failed to realize the significance of the experiences other people have had in the park at Versailles. The Crooke family, for instance, saw the 'sketching lady' observed by Miss Moberly but not by Miss Jourdain. Mrs Gregory saw a woman shaking a white cloth out of the window of a building, as did Miss Moberly. Miss Moberly and Miss Jourdain saw two men dressed in a green uniform; the old man seen by Miss Burrow and Miss Lambert in 1928 also wore a green uniform. In 1770 Claude Richard, the royal gardener, was 65. Miss Burrow said that the man she and Miss Lambert saw was 'sixty-ish'.

The 'adventure' of Miss Moberly and Miss Jourdain in 1901 is most unusual in that they were able to communicate in their dreamlike experience with the ghostly figures they met. Nor was this confined to these two ladies only; Miss Burrow and Miss Lambert in their encounter with the old man also heard him answer their request for information about the Trianon by shouting 'sentence after sentence in hoarse and unintelligible French'. Just as Miss Burrow and Miss Lambert had trouble in understanding what the old man said, Miss Moberly and Miss Jourdain had the same difficulty in their encounters; they found the words of those who spoke to them 'extraordinarily difficult to catch'. This is a common experience in dreams. In nearly all the accounts of retrocognitive experiences I have studied, the observers have been confined to the role of spectators and have not been able to communicate with those taking part in the drama.

Some happening in the past seems to have left its imprint on the Petit Trianon and its surroundings and I was puzzled by what it could be, particularly as the experience of Miss Moberly and Miss Jourdain related to a time before the outbreak of the Revolution and its subsequent terror. As I remarked in my first study of the Versailles case in *The Unexplained*:

> What I cannot explain is why these hallucinatory experiences seem to apply to one particular period and not a dramatic one at that. The shadow of the Revolution had not yet fallen across France. There is a theory in psychical research that cases of telepathy, clairvoyance, or of the appearance of apparitions involve an agent and a percipient or an agent-percipient. If this is so, who was the long-dead agent who presumably left some influence on the Trianons which could, in certain atmospheric conditions, 'trigger off' the hallucinatory experiences of certain visitors to the gardens in modern time?
>
> (1966: 88)

A possible answer to this question came over twenty years later from the author Jean Overton Fuller who, in a letter in the April 1990 issue of the SPR *Journal*, said:

My mother was a person with very strong reactions to places. Some she would not go near. Usually, retrospective research into the background of a place where she had been paralysed by terror afforded some reason to imagine it might have been anciently a site of Druidic human sacrifice. That did not explain her dislike and fear of Versailles. Her father had, since his second marriage, gone to live in it [Versailles]. I cannot deny that she may already have read the *Adventure*, but the impression created by its authors was not sinister, and I have heard her refer to the book with pleasant interest. Her dread was of the place itself. In 1928, when I was thirteen, we were invited. I knew Mother did not want to go, only she could think of no reason to refuse, as we were passing through Paris. after lunch, inevitably, we were taken into the Château and its gardens. My grandfather, Col. Frederick Smith, RAMC, loved it. In 1914 he had commandeered the Hotel Trianon as the No. 4 Letter A General Hospital in France, and he walked down the grand avenue as if he belonged there, stopping to suggest to a gardener the treatment for an ailing bush. Mother managed to put on a smiling face until we reached the Petit Trianon. They wanted to take us in, and here she stuck her feet in as though resisting being pulled, and refused absolutely to go in or a step further towards it. Her revulsion and fear were most evident, and we had to come away.

In the station, after we had settled into our carriage, there was still a delay of a few minutes before the train pulled out. I looked at Mother. She appeared still to be suffering from the ill-effects of the place. Guessing at the way in which her thoughts were running, I said: 'They weren't executed here.'

She flashed back at me, 'It was here their melancholy thoughts returned while they were waiting to be executed.'

I feel that the above account provides an excellent example of the 'imprint' theory as it concerns retrocognition and the feedback from it obtained at certain places by sensitive people. Miss Fuller's mother was obviously extremely sensitive to the atmosphere of certain spots; at some, as her daughter pointed out, she was 'paralysed by terror' and she dreaded going to Versailles. The reason for this was the overwhelming feeling of sadness she sensed there, because it was to Versailles that King Louis XVI's thoughts, and those of his queen, Marie Antoinette, were directed while they were in prison awaiting execution. It was these thoughts that had been imprinted on the park and mansion to create an atmosphere that was fed back to those sensitive enough to receive it. This feedback induced depression in some; in Miss Fuller's mother it induced terror.

Chapter 5

A Review

All four cases given above contain veridical elements. I have dwelt at some length on the one distinctive detail in Chapter 1 – the butcher's shop with decaying meat in it – the site of which Mr Laing was able to indicate on a postcard of the village he sent back to me from Australia. There may, of course, have been another butcher's shop in another part of the village at the time indicated by the visionary experience of Mr Laing and his companions but, even so, it is remarkable that he was able to indicate a house at a spot where a butcher's shop once stood.

Chapter 2 contains Mr John Watson's account of how he saw, as a schoolboy, a Nottingham street, Jessamine Cottages, as it was before it was demolished five years earlier. As he admits, he could have seen this street when he was a child, and forgotten the fact, but, even so, his experience was a remarkable one. There is no doubt that the street he 'saw' once stood in the place where he had seen it; he described it to his mother, as she confirms, and to others, and he searched for it without success. It is significant that a local writer said that 'the cottages can be passed in Castle Road without notice'. This lessens the likelihood that Mr Watson could have seen them during his rambles as a schoolboy. I find this account particularly convincing from an evidential viewpoint.

When Mrs McAvoy went to see her crofter friends at Altandhu (Chapter 3) there were no ruins or indications of a dwelling to trigger off the vision of the house that she 'saw', but which was no longer there when she tried to point it out to her husband after he called for her, as he confirmed in his note. Here crofter friends later confirmed that a house once stood on the spot she described.

It should be accepted, from the evidence advanced in Chapter 4, that certain features of the park of the Petit Trianon as described by Miss Moberly and Miss Jourdain, could be fitted into the scene as it was in 1770–71 but not, as they thought, in their obsession with Marie Antoinette, as it was in 1789, by which time many of the features of the grounds as they were when the old King, Louis XV, reigned, had been removed.

What of the people who had these experiences?

It is significant that most of the principal witnesses in the cases given here had psychical gifts and had had other psychical experiences. In their 'answers to questions which we have been asked' Miss Moberly and Miss Jourdain said in *An Adventure* that 'one of us has to own to having powers of second sight, etc., deliberately undeveloped, and there are psychical gifts in her family. She comes of Huguenot stock' (Miss Jourdain). The passage continues:

> The other [Miss Moberly] is one of a large and cheerful party, being the seventh daughter and of a seventh son; her mother and grandmother were entirely Scotch, and both possessed powers of premonition accompanied by vision. Her family has always been sensitive to ghost stories in general, but mercilessly critical of particular ones of a certain type. Both of us have inherited a horror of all forms of occultism. We lose no opportunity of preaching against them as unwholesome and misleading; because they mostly deal with conditions of physical excitement, and study of the abnormal and diseased, including problems of disintegrated personality which present such close analogy to those of insanity. We have the deepest distrust in, and distaste for, stories of abnormal appearances and conditions . . . . We have never had the curiosity, or the desire, to help in the investigations of psychical phenomena.
>
> (1955: 85)

Mr Laing, when a naval radio operator in 1961, saw what he believed to be the apparition of a Women's Royal Naval Service officer in an underground, high security passage at a naval headquarters in Scotland. Mr Watson, who 'saw' the vanished street in Nottingham in 1961 when he was a schoolboy, had the strange experience of seeing a man dressed as a cavalier or highwayman at the side of a road when driving in a motor rally in January 1967, although his navigator and his mother, who was a passenger in the back seat, saw nothing. Mrs McAvoy, who 'saw' the long-vanished house at Altandhu, wrote to me that 'ESP is a subject that fascinates me, and, looking back, something that has always been in many small ways a part of my life – and beliefs – starting no doubt from my mother's rather matter-of-fact habit of sending telepathic messages to my father from our home to his office, a matter of some twenty miles should she want to remind him of anything'. My correspondent had an unnerving experience in a house at Altandhu reputed to be haunted although this did not involve seeing an apparition.

It should not be thought from this that my correspondents named above fall into that small proportion of the population classified by psychologists as 'fantasy prone' and given to 'seeing things'. People of that type do not usually have experiences containing veridical elements. Judging from my postbag it is not unusual for sensitive people of a certain personality structure to have several experiences of a psychical nature during a lifetime.

Let us now consider the circumstances in which the experiences outlined above took place and the states of mind of the various percipients. It was a quiet Sunday morning when Mr Laing and his two companions from HMS *Ganges* set off on their trek across the fields in 1957 and some three hours later, according to Mr Crowley, when they reached the village. The only people they saw on the way were the surly cottager and his family. The village itself was deserted. Mr Laing wrote in one of his early letters that 'There was a complete silence and it was a dead natureless [unnatural?] silence (most noticeable to me as a Highland Scot used to country life). We did feel rather nonplussed at first as well as nervous, it all seemed so eerie, but I felt that flat empty feeling of depression which lifted after going back through the fields.' He also noticed the unnatural appearance of the trees and the sudden transformation of the hues of autumn outside the village to the springlike green inside it.

In Mr Watson's experience (Chapter 2) he was 'strolling aimlessly' round Nottingham when he turned a corner 'and was suddenly struck with a feeling of having stepped into the past', as indeed he had. There was no one in sight and the street was 'surprisingly quiet for somewhere near a city centre'. Mrs Woodhouse, who used to live in one of the cottages in the street, considered that, as the majority of the cottages were occupied by elderly people most of the time, the row of cottages would appear deserted, but in Mr Watson's opinion the most striking thing about Jessamine Cottages 'was not so much the fact that it was deserted but more the silence of it'. It is significant, I feel, that at the time of his experience Mr Watson was 'wandering aimlessly'. At such a time his mind would be open to impressions.

When Mrs Gladys McAvoy set out to visit her crofter friends in Altandhu (Chapter 3) she was alone, except for the dog, was feeling very 'vague', which she attributed to fatigue, and was 'pleasantly relaxed'. She wrote that 'no one was about' but as she was in a remote Highland village the absence of people could be expected. It was a place that had a 'wonderful peace and "other worldliness" that seems to change the nature of time'. An interesting point resulting from Mrs McAvoy's account was that her crofter friends believed she had had her experience because 'someone is thinking of building there', as indeed was the case. In other words, there was a telepathic explanation for the experience, with the crofter-postman as agent. Possibly this was so, but the telepathic theory cannot as easily be invoked for incidents of the type described in this book as it can, say, for examples of crisis apparitions, when it is quite reasonable to assume that a person undergoing a crisis concentrates on a loved one who 'picks up' the thought and externalizes the impression in the form of an apparition or the scene where the crisis is taking place. However, Mr G. W. Lambert believed that the agent in the Versailles case could have been the younger Richard, Antoine, who succeeded his father as royal gardener and whose plan for the English garden was rejected by the queen in favour of one by a gifted amateur gardener, the Comte de Caraman. Antoine Richard must have been deeply hurt by this decision and could have brooded on it.

When Miss Burrow and Miss Lambert visited the gardens of the Petit Trianon in 1928 they were overcome by feelings of depression. The solicitor's wife who went with her husband to the Trianons in 1955 felt 'unaccountably depressed'. They had seen no one since leaving the Grand Trianon to pass through the grounds of the Petit Trianon on the way to Marie Antoinette's village. The Wilkinson family were alone in the park, so far as they knew, in 1949 when they saw the figure of a woman in the costume of an earlier period on the top of the steps of the Grand Trianon. There was, said Mr Wilkinson, 'a noticeable quiet and stillness about the place'.

Miss Moberly and Miss Jourdain had felt depressed during their visit to the park in 1901 and in their preface to the fourth edition of *An Adventure* in 1931 they said that 'The chief features of our experience on that pleasant afternoon were the impressions of exceptional loneliness, and the extreme silence and stillness of the place'.

If we assume, as I feel we must, that all those who took part in the experiences related here were hallucinated, it seems that the trancelike state is often accompanied by feelings of depression, eeriness and a marked sense of silence, deeper than that normally experienced. Such experiences may be shared; a significant proportion of those given here may be classified as collective hallucinations.

Sane people who are in good health may not know that they are hallucinating. For instance, Miss Moberly and Miss Jourdain wrote that 'Though on the afternoon of our first visit to the Petit Trianon there were moments of oppression, yet we were not asleep, nor in a trance, nor even greatly surprised – everything was too natural. Astonishment came later, when we knew more.' What the two ladies did not understand was that during an experience involving hallucination everything can seem entirely natural. Mrs Sidgwick, in her early review of *An Adventure* in the SPR *Proceedings*, does not refer to hallucinations, apart from 'supposed hallucinatory music heard by Miss Jourdain on a subsequent visit in 1902'. Mr Sturge-Whiting did not think they were hallucinated, but other commentators have considered that they were. In his study of the case in the SPR *Journal* for July 1953 Mr Lambert said:

> It seems to me that in the narratives of the two observers there are unmistakable indications that on 10 August they were both deeply hallucinated as to sight and hearing, practically all the way from the gardener's house, where they entered the garden, until they entered the House. Apart from the fact that they saw objects which they could not afterwards find or satisfactorily identify, they described some in terms that are revealing to the student of parapsychology. I am assured by one who knew both the observers well that they did not suffer from any noticeable degree of short or defective sight. They could be relied upon to describe with reasonable accuracy anything they had seen in the course of a walk through a garden.
>
> (1953: 131)

Mr Lambert continues:

Assuming that the two were hallucinated, what was the 'mechanism' of the process? I think that the best way to picture it is to imagine that in front of the eyes of the subject a pair of spectacles is placed. The lenses are cut away at the bottom, so that the subject can look down his nose and see in the ordinary way his feet and enough of the immediate surroundings for him to walk about without straying or walking into obstacles. But when he raises his eyes and looks through the lenses, he sees not the ordinary field of vision but a 'spectral' field, the objects of which are subject to what one might call 'the laws of dreams'. While the subject is looking 'through the lenses', a 'part' of him is watching his steps all the time, and keeping an eye on his safety (as in the case of sleep-walkers). Let us call this part the Monitor. If the subject hesitates through indecision, or is running into danger, the Monitor can send a signal to the dreaming self which is for the time being conscious. The signal can take the form of a 'hunch' to go on, to stop, or to turn aside, as the case may be, or it may be externalized into the spectral field of vision as a symbolic figure, giving directions or the like in a more or less dramatic manner. This simile of spectacles is of course too mechanical to be accurate. The 'lenses' seem to form themselves and to melt away quite rapidly. While they are forming at the onset of hallucination, and melting away at the end of the period, curious optical effects are liable to be noticed by the subject. At the onset white objects in the spectral field show up first, and white objects in the normal field are the first to show signs of being suffused by the spectral field.

(1953: 133)

Mr Lambert pointed out that 'the most compelling evidence that the observers were hallucinated lies in what they did *not* see. During the whole of that walk, lasting perhaps half an hour, only eight persons were seen . . . . This was on 10 August, when the number of visitors to the garden must have been large.' I agree that this was almost certainly so, particularly as when the two ladies went to the Petit Trianon on a Monday and a Saturday in July 1904, they came across in every corner 'groups of noisy merry people walking or sitting in the shade. Garden seats placed everywhere, and stall for fruit and lemonade took away from any idea of desolation.' Miss Moberly had 'not expected such complete disillusionment'.

A Review

It is a reasonable assumption that on a fine Saturday afternoon in August there would have been a large number of people in the gardens of the Petit Trianon but they were excluded from the visionary experience, with the details of the park as it was in 1901. A comparison may be made in this connection with the experience of Mr Laing and his companions on a Sunday morning in Kersey in the autumn of 1957. They saw no one, indoors or out, although they peered in a number of windows. Late on a Sunday morning people would be coming home from church, although no church was visible to the visitors, or going to the two pubs that were certainly there in fact but were not included in the hallucinatory experience. People in the street must certainly have seen the three lads from HMS *Ganges* in 1957, and strollers in the grounds of the Petit Trianon on that Saturday afternoon in 1901 must have seen Miss Moberly and Miss Jourdain during their walk to the house. I discussed this point during my correspondence with Mr Laing. He wrote: 'People in 1957 must have seen us walking though Kersey dressed in blue naval shirts and blue trousers and boots.'

When the experience of the little party from HMS *Ganges* in Kersey in 1957 is compared with that of Miss Moberly and Miss Jourdain in Versailles in 1901 it will be seen that they have a number of features in common. Those taking part in the experiences were hallucinated to the extent that people of the present day were excluded and the scenery of the past was substituted for that of the present; all felt unaccountably depressed; there was an air of exceptional stillness and mystery, also fear, and the trees had an unnatural appearance. However, there were distinctive elements in both experiences. Miss Moberly and Miss Jourdain communicated with spectral figures – there were none such in Kersey – and in Kersey there was the strange transformation of the seasons from autumn in the fields outside to spring in the village itself. If it is argued, as some critics have, that all the supposed eighteenth-century persons described in the book might have been met in the flesh in the Versailles of 1901 then we have to explain the behaviour of some of them. The running man, for instance, came 'over, round, or through' the rock and the chapel man came out of a door that, in 1901, had been closed for many years.

Critics of Miss Moberly's and Miss Jourdain's Versailles 'adventure' have made much of the fact that the two ladies presented their evidence in an unsatisfactory way. As Dr Evans has pointed out in her foreword to *The Trianon Adventure*: 'They planned and tackled their researches in an amateurish way, with little sense of the relative value of primary and secondary evidence, and a very sketchy idea of such fundamentals as the organization of the French royal household.' However, it does not follow that because the evidence for an experience is presented badly the experience could not have taken place. One of the most perceptive comments on the Versailles case I have come across is that made by Aniela Jaffé in *Apparitions and Precognition: A Study from the Point of View of C. G. Jung's Analytical Psychology*:

One of the most interesting cases recorded in parapsychological literature is the adventure of Miss Moberly and Miss Jourdain, two schoolmistresses who, in 1901, witnessed at the Petit Trianon, Versailles, scenes from the life of Marie Antoinette just before her imprisonment (1799) [surely 1789?] and even took a 'speaking part' in them. The inexplicable depression, the state of dreaminess, recorded by both women during their adventure definitely points to the state of diminished consciousness which is the necessary condition for the occurrence of phenomena of the kind.

It is inevitable that their adventure should become a target for the cross-fire of opinions. Lucille Iremonger's book *The Ghosts of Versailles* is not only an excellent guide to the pros and cons of the judgements which have been passed since the original publication, but her character sketches of the two women shows the weaknesses, the ambition and the romanticism of these intelligent 'old spinsters'. Yet even Mrs Iremonger has not succeeded in unmasking *An Adventure* as a pure fabrication, and she leaves readers to form their own judgement.

One of the principal charges brought by the critics is that the accounts of the adventure were first written down three months after the experience. It is, however, a fact that such strange and rare occurrences leave a deep imprint on the human mind, they become a lasting possession and remain vivid for years afterwards. We may note the doubts cast on the authenticity of the story, and also imagine that certain details of this rich and strange experience, in which a number of persons 'appeared', were not rendered with absolute fidelity; further that one of the participants was unconsciously influenced by what the other had seen and inserted it into her account later. But we must question whether in such an experience the faithful photographic or phonographic reproduction of all details is the main point. It must rather be emphasized that Miss Moberly and Miss Jourdain felt they had 'entered into another age'. Their description of the immediate circumstances shows that they were in that state of diminished consciousness in which a relativization of time and space may occur. Time was, as it were, extended into the past.

(1963: 120–23)

This accords with Stephen Hawking's statement, quoted in the Preface, that the laws of science did not distinguish between the forward and backward directions of time.

In the second part of this book we consider cases of a varying type, each of which is greatly instructive of how phenomena of the type under discussion may be interpreted. Some, thought to be examples of retrocognition and reported as such, proved on investigation to have a natural explanation; others, despite intensive research, have remained mysterious. In some cases, although a natural explanation has been provided, puzzling features still remain. While considering the cases that follow, and in assessing those in the first part of the book, we must keep in mind the rule that a natural cause for seemingly mysterious phenomena must be sought before a paranormal one can be advanced.

PART TWO

Puzzling and controversial cases

Chapter 6

Spectral Houses

Reports of spectral houses are always of particular interest because there is the possibility, discussed in more detail in the next chapter, that the house may, in fact, exist and if a sufficiently careful search is made may eventually be located. In this chapter I will relate accounts of unsuccessful searches for such houses, leaving us in little doubt that the buildings and surrounding described in detail never existed.

The first house so described was at the rambling village of Bradfield St George near Bury St Edmunds in Suffolk. This account is taken from Sir Ernest Bennett's *Apparitions and Haunted Houses* (1939), based on reports he received after making a broadcast on apparitions and haunted houses in March 1934. It was sent to him by Miss Ruth Wynne, who is remembered in the district as an accomplished young woman who ran a small private school at nearby Rougham Rectory; she seems to have begun with a single pupil. In her letter to Sir Ernest she said:

> I came to live at Rougham, four miles from Bury St Edmunds, in 1926. The district was then entirely new to me, and I and my pupil, a girl of fourteen, spent our afternoon walks exploring it.
>
> One dull, damp afternoon, I think in October '26, we walked off through the fields to look at the church of the neighbouring village, Bradfield St George. In order to reach the church, which we could see plainly ahead of us to the right, we had to pass through a farmyard, whence we came out on to a road. We had never previously taken this particular walk, nor did we know anything about the topography of the hamlet of Bradfield St George. Exactly opposite us on the further side of the road and flanking it, we saw a high wall of greenish-yellow bricks. The road ran past us for a few yards, then curved away from us to the left. We walked along the road, following the brick

71

wall round the bend, where we came upon tall, wrought-iron gates set in the wall. I think the gates were shut, or one side may have been open. The wall continued on from the gates and disappeared round the curve of the road.

Behind the wall and towering above it was a cluster of tall trees. From the gates, a drive led away among these trees to what was evidently a large house. We could just see a corner of the roof above a stucco front in which I remember noticing some windows of Georgian design. The rest of the house was hidden by the branches of the trees.

We stood by the gates for a moment, speculating as to who lived in this large house, and I was rather surprised that I had not already heard of the owner amongst the many people who had already called on my mother since our arrival in the district. This house was one of the nearest large residences to our own, and it seemed odd that the occupants had not called. However, we then turned off the road along a footpath leading away to the right of the church which was perhaps under a hundred yards off. On leaving the church, we cut through the churchyard into the fields and home, without returning to the road or to the farmyard. It was then drizzling rain.

On arriving home, we discussed the big house and its possible occupants with my parents, and then thought no more of it.

My pupil and I did not take the same walk again until the following spring. It was, as far as I can remember, a dull afternoon with good visibility in February or March. We walked up through the farmyard as before, and out on to the road, where, suddenly, we both stopped dead of one accord and gasped. 'Where's the wall?' we queried simultaneously. It was not there. The road was flanked by nothing but a ditch, and beyond the ditch lay a wilderness of tumbled earth, weeds, mounds, all overgrown with the trees which we had seen on our first visit.

We followed the road on round the bend but there were no gates, no drive, no corner of the house to be seen. We were both very puzzled. At first we thought that our house and wall had been pulled down since our last visit. But closer inspection showed a pond and other small pools amongst the mounds where the house had been visibly. It was obvious that they had been there a long time.

Yet, we were both independently certain that we had seen

the house and wall on our previous visit, and our recollections coincided exactly. I should mention that my pupil was neither imaginative nor suggestible, and that we were sufficiently good friends to permit her to disagree with me firmly had she wished to do so.

We then returned home, half amused, half bothered, and yet convinced that we *had* seen that wall and house on the occasion of our first visit. We mentioned the matter to my parents, who, although not altogether incredulous, thought that we must have been mistaken. They don't think so now. Later, I made various tentative inquiries of some villagers who lived near the site of our mystery, but they had never heard of a house existing at that spot, and obviously thought my question a foolish one, so I let the matter drop.

I have not yet succeeded in finding an eighteenth-century map of that district, but I am convinced still that the house either once stood there, or else I shall meet it again somewhere else. I have often been past its site since, but I have never seen it again. The matter has puzzled me ever since and I would be grateful if any light could be thrown on the experience.

I am not what might be called psychic and this is the only experience of the kind that I have ever had.

The pupil alluded to in Miss Wynne's letter was Miss Allington of Lady Margaret Hall Settlement, south-east London. She wrote to Sir Ernest in February 1937 as follows:

I am sorry to say that the incident has become somewhat blurred by the lapse of time, but here is our experience as far as I can remember it. Miss Wynne and I were going for the usual daily walk, and happened to choose a footpath leading to Bradfield St George. We were both new to that part of the world, and it was the first time we had taken this walk. We passed the church and Rectory, and came out on to a road, just an ordinary country by-road, and saw opposite us an old brick wall. Behind the wall could be seen trees, and obviously, a house. I can't remember the details of the house, but I remember discussing with Miss Wynne who could be living there. Next time we took the same walk, we came to the road at the same spot, but no trace of the wall could be seen. I thought it very strange, and wondered if

I had mistaken the spot, as we were comparatively new to the neighbourhood; but Miss Wynne asked me at once where the wall had got to, as she had obviously expected to see it there, as I had also. We never saw it again, and in the four years that I was in those parts, I got to know the country well. There was quite definitely no wall in the neighbourhood like the one we saw, so it could not be a case of a mistake in our way.

(1939: 563)

Sir Ernest Bennett, MP, a member of the council of the SPR, died in 1947. Commenting on this case, he said:

The vision of the Georgian mansion is unique in this collection [of 103 cases] and reminds one of the well-known 'Trianon' experience of Miss Moberly and Miss Jourdain. It may at first sight appear impossible that no recollection or tradition should exist today of an imposing Georgian mansion, had this formerly existed in a village. But the perpetual drift from the countryside to the towns, and the decimation of a whole generation in the Great War, are factors which have rudely shaken the former continuity of village tradition. Church registers and tombstones are often the only reliable evidence for the existence of houses and families in rural England which otherwise have lived without a history and perished without a memorial; and if research along these or other lines revealed the fact that a large house did once stand on the site indicated in the story the case would be one of singular interest and importance.

The case is still one of singular interest and importance as an example of a collective hallucination, but inquiries I have made in the district and at the Bury St Edmunds branch of the Suffolk Record Office have revealed that no such house ever existed. The 1843 tithe map showed that the land described above belonged to the Rev. Robert Davers, rector of the local church, and contained at that time a large round plantation, a pond, and a smaller plantation near the corner where the road curved. Mr Leonard Aves, a local historian, discussing the case in a booklet of which he is joint author with his wife, said that the only building in this area of any consequence, shown in the tithe map of 1843, was Bradfield Hall, the site of which Miss Wynne would have passed on leaving the farmyard. Bradfield Hall was demolished in the 1850s.

1. The approach to Kersey from the East. The author (left) studies his notes.

2. Looking up the hill towards the church from the water splash.

3. The water splash at Kersey.

4. The Bell Inn at Kersey. It was invisible during Mr Laing's experience in 1957.

5. Mr Laing stands in front of the house which was once a butcher's shop at Kersey.

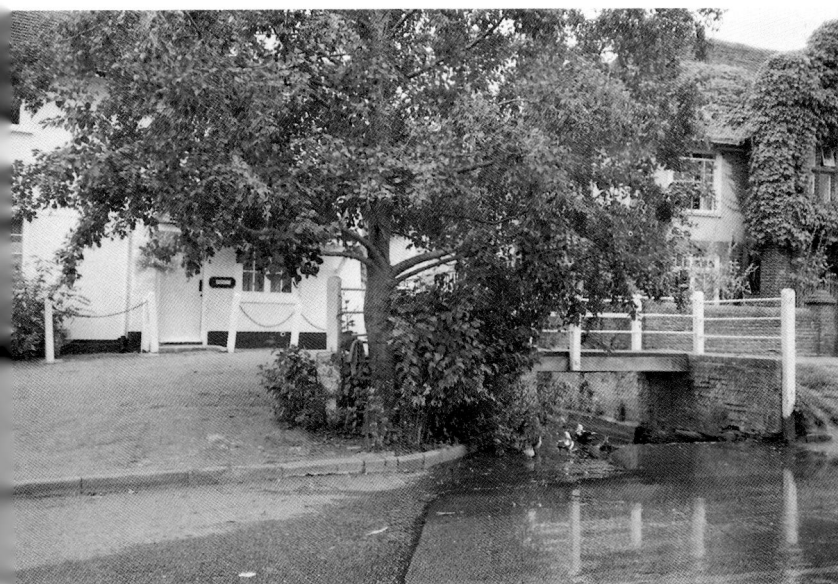

6. The modern bridge over the water splash at Kersey is overshadowed by the tree. The house which was once a butcher's shop is on the left of the bridge.

7. If Mr John Watson, or anyone else, looked at the scene shown here they would certainly not see old fashioned cottages and flowers which he saw during his experience (Chapter 7).

With a friend I stood on the spot from which Miss Wynne and her pupil gazed at the high wall and house beyond in 1926 and surveyed what was indeed a wilderness of tall trees, mounds, a pond with rushes and weeds, merging into meadows, behind a wide ditch. The scene was much the same as that described by Miss Wynne on her second visit except that now there was a small modern house near the corner of the road. The wall hallucinated by Miss Wynne and her pupil must have extended for 300 yards or more.

Strangely enough, there is a tradition of disappearing houses at Bradfield St George. An account in the issue of *Amateur Gardening* of 20 December 1975 by a Mr James Cobbold (pseudonym) told how, around 1860, in the Kingshall Street area his great-grandfather Robert Palfrey, a local resident, was just putting the finishing touches to a haystack he was thatching when he happened to look over the narrow lane and there stood a house and garden with roses and flower-beds in full bloom. The house had solid red bricks and the flower-beds were edged with the same red bricks planted slantwise and half buried. There were two entrances with ornamental iron gates, which were closed. Mr Palfrey was frightened and puzzled. Although it was a warm June evening, the atmosphere had turned distinctly chilly, conveying the impression of something unreal. When he returned home that night he related what he had seen and with his relatives went back to the spot, only to find that the house and garden had disappeared.

Mr Cobbold had his own experience of a phantom house as a boy. He used to go out with a butcher, Mr George Waylett, on his Saturday deliveries round the district. They had just left one of his calls in Kingshall Street and were jogging along nicely towards Bradfield St George when there was a loud swishing 'whoosh' as of air displacement, the air became very cold, the pony reared and bolted, and Mr Waylett was thrown from the cart. In those fleeting moments Mr Cobbold most distinctly saw a double-fronted, red-brick house roofed with pantiles, three-storeyed, of pronounced Georgian appearance. In front were flower-beds in full bloom. Mr Cobbold managed to stop the pony and turned it round, since he feared for Mr Waylett. Even as he did so, 'a kind of mist seemed to envelop the house, which I could still see, and the whole thing simply disappeared, it just went'. Fortunately, Mr Waylett was not much hurt.

Mr Cobbold was 12-years-old at the time. Ignoring a warning

from Mr Waylett not to go near, he scrambled through the hedge into the field where the house and garden had been so plainly visible. He said, 'I expected to see at least crushing of the young spring corn where this house had stood. There was no trace; nothing but the vigorous young wheat, shortly to be in ear. I remember being just as scared at this sign of nothing as I had been of the actual phenomenon.' Mr Waylett had told him that this was the third time he had seen the house appear and disappear.

After the *Amateur Gardening* article appeared, a young man from the village told Mr Cobbold that his father had seen the same happening at least twice during the past ten years (1965–75).

Mr Cobbold was interviewed by Mr and Mrs Aves and a Captain D. Armstrong RN of Rougham, having come back from Cambridgeshire, where he then lived, for that purpose. From Rougham he took them southwards along Kingshall Street to a point by Gypsy Lane. On the opposite side of the road there was a gap in the hedgerow with an entrance to the field, then in winter wheat. Very firmly, and with no hint an any hesitation, Mr Cobbold indicated a point in the field, about 30 yards in, nearly in line with the northern end of Colville's Grove. 'It was there', he declared. It was the identical spot where his great-grandfather had seen the house when hs was thatching the stack on the other side of the street in 1860. I estimate that Mr Cobbold's experience took place in 1908. The hallucination lasted, he estimated, between eight and ten minutes.

Mrs Doris Aves told me that Kingshall Street is about half a mile from the spot where Miss Wynne and Miss Allingham had their experience.

I think that possibly two phantom houses are involved in the experiences at Bradfield St George. The one seen by Miss Wynne and Miss Allington gave the impression of being a mansion but that seen by Mr Cobbold had, he estimated, the frontage of two council houses, less than 60 feet.

An account of another brick wall, seen collectively, was contained in a letter from Mr Kenneth E. Bull, a retired bookseller, then of Tunbridge Wells, Kent. The experience was on 21 September 1978, when, with his wife, he was staying at Bridgnorth, Salop. They caught a bus out from Bridgnorth to a little village a couple of miles out, to visit a church. After this they decided to walk back to Bridgnorth by a quiet little lane.

It was a sunny, quite day, and we did not see a soul anywhere. We passed a sign saying 'Boldings Farm', and almost at once, down the lane ahead of us, I saw a low red-brick wall, seeming to slant across the road. Knowing that the disused railway was on our left, running parallel with the road, I at once said: 'Looks as if that's a railway bridge', and my wife agreed. But a second or two later, at the end of the wall, there came into view what seemed to be a tall building, also of mellow red brick, and roofless. So I then exclaimed: 'No, it's not a bridge, looks like a ruined farmhouse or something of that sort.' After that we took our eye 'off the ball' for a few seconds; we are both botanists, and presumably were looking at the roadside. When we looked down the lane again there was nothing there at all. We couldn't believe it. We went much further down the lane, then retraced our steps right back to Boldings Farm, but there was no sign of a building anywhere near the road, nor any foundations. I had the feeling, rightly or wrongly, that we must have seen a ruined building that had stood there in the past.

It later transpired that Mrs Bull had seen the brick wall very distinctly but not the building at the end of it. Mr Bull wrote to the owner of Boldings Farm to ask if a building had once stood on the spot where he had seen it but did not get a reply. I suggested that he made inquiries at the local library at Bridgnorth. The librarian there replied that a number of 6-inch Ordnance Survey maps from 1842 to 1954 had been examined but the library staff were unable to find any evidence of a building that stood 200 yards south of Boldings Farm.

It seems that Mr and Mrs Bull hallucinated the wall and Mr Bull the building and it is unlikely that what they had seen had ever existed. I have had many reports describing how the act of looking away from a person or an object is sufficient to make it disappear because of the change in the state of consciousness. It is significant that Mr Bull commented on the quietness and that they 'did not see a soul anywhere'.

An example of yet another Georgian house seen collectively, this time near Hadleigh, Essex, was given by the late Mrs Rosalind Heywood, a gifted writer and sensitive, in the December 1961 *Journal* of the SPR. Her informant was Miss Grace MacMahon who wrote to her in the hope, she said, of finding some reason for an experience which had greatly puzzled her. Miss MacMahon wrote as follows:

> One morning my brother and I went for a walk from Leigh-on-Sea, where we lived, to a creek near Hadleigh, mooring place for a couple of dozen houseboats. Our walk led us along the edge of a wood. This wood we had explored many times before.
>
> Halfway along the path we were astonished to see a clearing in the wood and a gravel drive leading up to an imposing Georgian house with an impressive drive. Hurrying down the drive toward us was a young girl with an Alsatian dog. The girl was dressed in contemporary clothes. They crossed our path and vanished over the hill quite normally. We could not recall ever having seen a house in the wood before but made little comment at the time.
>
> When we arrived at our friends' houseboat we told them of the house in the wood. They assured us that no such house existed. My brother and I were so positive that there was a house in the woods that we all tramped back to have a look at it. We travelled from one end of the path to the other. House, drive had gone. Over and over we repeated that we had seen a house in the wood, but at last we gave up looking for it. After spending many hours since then searching these woods, and looking up old books and records in the libraries, going over maps, and questioning many local people, we can find no evidence that there has ever been a house in the wood. But there was a house because my brother and I saw it.

Miss MacMahon afterwards came to see Mrs Heywood and made a sketch map from which Mrs Heywood was able to locate the exact spot on an Ordnance Survey map of the district. Miss MacMahon added that the girl walked along a track across the railway on her way over the hill and that she had since found out that this track was a disused one from a brick kiln which had been shut down many years ago. She said that her brother, Mr Bruce James MacMahon, an engineer, was extremely sceptical about such matters but she would ask him to add his confirmation to her account. This he did by signing with his sister the following statement: 'This is to confirm that my brother and I saw the house at Hadleigh fifteen years ago – and have not had a similar experience since.' The experience probably took place in the mid-1940s.

This case was followed up by Mr G. W. Lambert who asked Mr R. G. H. Andrews, a member of the SPR who lived in the neighbourhood, to check on it. Mr Andrews and his wife studied several maps in the borough engineer's office at the municipal buildings, Southend-on-Sea, and others in the reference department of the central library there, this being the local authority in charge of the area where the Georgian house was seen. On these maps were shown the positions of the old brickworks, the old railway track belonging to the brickworks, and the creeks where the houseboats used to be moored just after the 1939–45 war. Nobody they spoke to in the borough engineer's office or the central library had ever heard of any house in the locality fitting Miss MacMahon's description and no house was shown on any of the maps they studied. Mr and Mrs Andrews made two prolonged visits to the area in question. They found evidence of the brickworks and parts of the disused line from a brick kiln. They saw several hills, over one of which the girl 'seen' by the MacMahons walked. The ruins of Hadleigh Castle were within this area, though on higher ground than where the MacMahons 'saw' the house in question. Most of the area was under the management of the Salvation Army farm colony at Hadleigh, much of it ploughed up as arable land the rest pasture. Mr and Mrs Andrews ended their report: 'We explored the area very thoroughly and *saw no evidence at all* of anything resembling "a gravel drive" or "an imposing Georgian house" as described by the MacMahons.'

The experience of Miss MacMahon and her brother remains a mystery.

Another example of a non-existent building was sent to me from Canada by Mrs Amy Meredith (pseudonym) who said that in the summer of 1981 while she was on a business trip to Edmonton (her first visit there) she saw a building which she immediately assumed to be the legislative building. She was in a taxi at the time, travelling along the freeway towards the building which sat at a sort of crossroads. 'It was a very large, impressive-looking building made of reddish brown bricks and it was sitting on a grassy knoll overlooking a beautiful wide blue river. As we rounded the bend in the road I was able to see it quite clearly over to the left and continued to look at it over my left shoulder for as long as it was visible. It was like a tableau. I felt elated and very excited and can recall thinking I didn't know Edmonton has anything as lovely as this.'

Mrs Meredith estimated that the building remained in her line of vision for approximately two minutes.

Then in 1985 she returned to Edmonton for a weeks' vacation with her son Tom (pseudonym) who was 14-years-old at the time and very eager to visit the West Edmonton Mall (the world's largest shopping mall). 'Well, as you can imagine I spoke to Tom at great length about Edmonton's beautiful legislative building and the impression it had made on me. Of course when I saw the real legislative building I was shocked and disappointed, extremely puzzled too. If this was the legislative building where could "my" building be?'

Since that time, said Mrs Meredith, she had been in touch with the Tourist Board of Edmonton, but people there had no knowledge of such a building. They had sent her many brochures, maps and pictures of Edmonton abut none of the buildings was anything like the one she saw. 'If I hadn't returned to Edmonton in '85 I would never have known that the building is not there. Which leads me to wonder how many people "see" buildings every day that aren't there in the physical sense, but they never realize it.'

Mrs Meredith's husband signed a statement that 'In the late summer of 1981, upon her return from Edmonton, I seem to have a vague recollection of Amy speaking about a building she had seen there. However, it was a long time ago, and although I've tried to remember the incident more clearly, I've been unable to recall any further details about it.'

Mrs Meredith commented: 'the experience did have a powerful effect on me, I can remember feeling quite excited and elated about the building and being so disappointed in 1985 when I couldn't find it again, I've always been very psychically sensitive when travelling. Physical, mental and emotional exhaustion, I suppose, leave the conscious mind not quite as vigilant as usual, giving the subconscious mind a freer rein. The heightened awareness that travel brings may also facilitate the process.'

Mrs Meredith was certain that she wasn't glimpsing a scene from Edmonton's past. 'If, however, this was a scene from another city's past, then why should it show up where it did? Perhaps it was not a scene from the past, but from another dimension? Or, in situations such as this, are we picking up on someone else's thought form?'

I am grateful to Mrs Meredith for sending me this interesting case. Her last questions, 'Are we picking up on someone else's thought form?', to account for her experience in seeing a non-existent building, will be discussed in the final chapter.

Chapter 7

Buildings Glimpsed in Passing

When people are on foot they have time to observe carefully their surroundings, and if they wish to check on a scene that they suspect may have been hallucinated they should have little difficulty in returning to the spot concerned to confirm their observations. Totally different conditions apply to observations made from a moving vehicle, particularly when one person in it, the driver, has to keep his or her eyes on the road. There is so little time for people in a car to fix a scene accurately in memory that later visits to a spot to establish whether a building seen in passing was hallucinated or actually existed are often unsuccessful. Two such cases are given in this chapter. They were first published as examples of collective hallucination in the *Journal* of the SPR. Publication resulted in investigators being alerted and it was as a result of their inquiries that solutions to the mysteries were found.

In June 1933, Mr Clifford Pye and his wife were on holiday at Falmouth. After being there for ten days they decided to spend the rest of the vacation on the north Cornish coast, the choice of locality being left to chance, though the general intention was to make first for Boscastle. On Saturday 17 June they went to Wadebridge by train, and there took a bus for Boscastle, passing Tintagel and subsequently Trevalga. They were then about a mile and a half from Boscastle and were keeping a good lookout for any hotel or guest house which might appear suitable.

On approaching Boscastle and at a point about 150 or 200 yards before reaching the top of the steep hairpin-bend hill which drops down into the town, the bus stopped momentarily to set down a passenger almost outside the gate of a rather substantial house on the left-hand side of the road. The house stood back from the road some 20 yards or so. The garden front was screened from the road by a hedge, over which Mr and Mrs Pye could just see from their seats in the bus. The house was double-fronted and of a style of architecture which Mr Pye judged to date from the late 1860s or early 1870s. It had a fresh, trim appearance, and seemed to have been recently painted, the woodwork and the quoins of the house being of a rather reddish light chocolate in colour. The most striking feature, however, was on the lawn, where among beds of scarlet geraniums there were several wicker or cane chairs and tables over which there were standing several large garden unbrellas of black and orange.

No person was seen. Mr Pye assumed that the building was a guest house. He drew his wife's attention to the place. She immediately replied that it was 'just what we were looking for', but before they could come to any decision the bus moved off and in two or three minutes they were down in Boscastle. Neither was attracted to the place, as they found the smell of seaweed on which a hot sun was shining disagreeable, so Mrs Pye volunteered to make inquiries at the place, assumed to be a guest house, they had passed at the top of the hill.

Mr Pye had expected his wife to return well within half an hour, but it was an hour and twenty-five minutes later when she came down the hill, looking considerably heated, to report that she had been unable to find the house, that she had climbed on various gates to look around but could see nothing, and so had continued until she got to Trevalga, a mile and a half away, where she had booked rooms.

Mr Pye said he could not understand how she had missed the house, the only detached one there, and pointed out that the umbrellas in the garden made it impossible to overlook the place. Mrs Pye was much astonished at her failure and could not understand how she had failed ot find the house. Mr Pye volunteered to point out the house to her on the return journey by bus. In his report to the SPR he said:

> In due course we got on this bus, and as we reached the top of the hill remarked, 'It's just here on the right – about fifty yards further on' – but to my astonishment there was no house. Just empty fields running across to the cliffs at Blackapit. During our stay at Trevalga we made a thorough search of the locality but failed to find any place even remotely resembling what we had

seen. On a subsequent visit to the Trevalga guest house I told our experience to the proprietor, who assured me that from his knowledge there was in the neighbourhood no such house as I described.

Mrs Pye made a separate statement.

The editor, in publishing the statements of Mr and Mrs Pye in the *Journal* for November–December 1942, said:

> There is the obvious possibility to be entertained that an actual house was seen and its locality incorrectly remembered, and on Cornish roads it is often easy to miss, when on foot, an object previously seen from a vehicle, owing to the height of the stone 'hedges'; but Mr and Mrs Pye seem to have been stirred by their mystification to make a very thorough search along the route they had previously traversed, before they could accept that a hallucination had misled them both.

The case was nine-years-old when it was published and it was another twenty years before a solution to the mystery was found. In the SPR *Journal* for March 1963 Mr G. W. Lambert told how he had persuaded Miss M. Scott-Eliott, a member of the society living in Devon, to search for the house which Mr and Mrs Pye were convinced they had hallucinated.

On 3 November 1962 with two friends she drove from Wadebridge to Boscastle via Tintagel and Trevalga. From Tintagel a careful lookout was kept on both sides of the road for a double-fronted detached house with lawn and drive as described by the Pyes. On the outskirts of Boscastle, halfway down the steep hill into the village, a house was seen that was in some ways similar to that described. It was on the left-hand side, was named Melbourne House, and at that time was being run as a private hotel.

A 12-foot wall and hedge hid the house from the road except when one turned the corner of the hill on the descent. Then for a brief moment a reasonably clear view was had of the house, lawn and drive, but the angle was such that the width of the drive in front of the house was not apparent. Miss Scott-Eliott had to back her car up the hill to the spot that gave the best view of the house and this then became more obvious than when they first passed the spot. On the ascent the angle of climb and the height of the hedge were such that the house was hardly visible.

The balcony and drainpipes were painted green. The inquirers were told at Melbourne House that the present owners had been there for some five or six years and that before that it was a private house owned and lived in by an old lady, the daughter of the man who had built it in 1861. The present owners never put chairs and tables outside and had never owned striped awnings or umbrellas.

Miss Scott-Eliott and her friends inquired at the post office and were given the name of the late owner's nephew who had lived with her and who, after his wife's death, sold the house. He was Mr E. W. Foster, a retired solicitor, then living at Trebarwith Strand. He told them that the woodwork of the house had originally been green but because the local hotel had been painted a rather vivid green Melbourne House was repainted brown. He could not remember when this was done but thought it was probably about 1932. He himself looked after the flower garden and always had the centre bed filled with scarlet geraniums. His father and mother, who lived in Somerset, made a practice of annually visiting Melbourne House in June and, as his mother particularly liked sitting outside if it was a fine day, tea was usually served outside on the drive. They never had any awning or umbrellas but the café at the foot of the hill did. It was the first local place, in fact, to have umbrellas and Mr Foster was fairly certain they were striped black and orange. The bus still stopped opposite the drive entrance.

Miss Scott-Eliott considered that Melbourne House must be the house the Pyes saw. The day of their visit was evidently a hot one as they found the smell of the seaweed oppressive. Mrs Foster would certainly have been staying at Melbourne House, and as it was a fine day tea would have been served in front of the house. Miss Scott-Eliott suggested that the chairs and tables put out in front of the house and only glimpsed by the Pyes, as their bus passed it, suggested to them that it was a guest house. The striped umbrellas, later seen at the café down the hill, were probably transferred in their minds to Melbourne House, and their failure to find the house again was because of its invisibility on ascending the hill on foot owing to the steepness of the ground and the height of the hedge. It was also likely that, if they did get a glimpse of it, Melbourne House, then a private house of some standing, looked much less like a boarding-house or hotel after the outside furniture had been removed. Mr Foster said that this was always done by the staff; things were never left outside.

Mr Lambert agreed that this was a case of mislocation, without any element of hallucination. It was very fortunate that Miss Scott-Eliott was able to make contact with Mr Foster so many years after the event and learn details about the appearance and surroundings of Melbourne House in 1933. Considering that the Pyes saw the house for only a few moments, and that they reported their experience about nine years after the event, their recollections seem to have been remarkable accurate. They included one interesting mistake. The orange and black garden umbrellas almost certainly belonged to the café some way past Melbourne House. This suggested that 'wrong' details get in from other mental images very closely associated *in time* with the main picture being recalled.

I agree with Mr Lambert's conclusion. What surprises me is that Mr and Mrs Pye did not realize the significance of the fact that there was a bus stop opposite the entrance to the house they were seeking. If they had, the house would have been speedily located.

The second case concerns a Mrs Peggy Fraser (pseudonym) who wrote to Mrs Rosalind Heywood to describe how, in November 1955, she and her husband decided to spend a weekend at a country hotel in Sussex, selected at random from a guidebook. They left London just after 6 p.m. on a Friday evening, but owing to torrential rain Mr Fraser drove slowly and it was nearly 7.30 when they approached Lower Dicker, where the road branched right to Eastbourne, and went straight ahead to Hastings. The receptionist had told Mr Fraser on the telephone that the hotel was a few miles south of Herstmonceux, and as they left the roundabout Mr Fraser said that they ought soon to be looking for it.

The rain was still beating down relentlessly and the Frasers had been travelling some ten minutes when, turning a gentle bend in the road, they saw on the left a lovely old country-house, lying back from the roadway some 25 years. Mr Fraser slowed down and they looked appreciatively at the hotel. It was covered with lichen and its windows were lighted with a diffused light that spoke of comfort and welcome. There was a gravel drive leading to the porticoed entrance and on the left was built a low, sloping-roofed addition with the words 'American bar' in neon lighting. Mrs Fraser said in her account: 'I can see as if it was only a moment ago the small red-shaded lamps and the bar and bottles and small inviting tables.'

'Do you think this is it?' Mrs Fraser asked hopefully, but her husband answered that it could not be as their hotel was on the right. She remarked that she hoped their hotel would be as nice as the one they had passed and he said they could go back there for a nightcap after dinner.

Shortly afterwards they reached their hotel and after dinner went back, this time with Mrs Fraser driving. She was a beginner and drove carefully all the way back to the roundabout at Lower Dicker. Mr Fraser said, 'That's funny, we must have missed it', and he took the wheel and they drove back again very slowly, looking out carefully. 'But the place had vanished. We also asked, but nothing was known of such a place.'

The Frasers talked of nothing else that weekend, and, said Mrs Fraser, 'My husband was annoyed, for he felt such a thing should not have happened to him of all people. Since that time we have made many journeys along that road to visit my parents in Hastings and each time we have looked for the hotel but we have never seen it again.'

Mr Fraser confirmed his wife's account.

Commenting on the case, which was published in the SPR *Journal* for December 1961, Mrs Heywood said: 'It is perhaps worth noting that Mr and Mrs Fraser appear to have seen such details as lichen on the roof more clearly than they would have done on a wet winter's evening had the house been an actual one.'

When Mr Denys Parsons, a well-known member of the SPR at the time, read the account he became convinced, by reason of the detailed nature of the description, that the Frasers had indeed seen such an hotel, and embarked with some confidence on a search for it, as he related in the SPR *Journal* for June 1962. He did not expect to find a building in the location indicated in the Frasers' account; he thought it likely that in the rain they had taken a wrong turning and had, for example, approached Herstmonceux on a parallel road. He spent an hour with the Ordnance maps in the local library, noting down the positions of all hotels within 5 miles of the road from Lower Dicker to Herstmonceux, and studying the local road system.

Mr Parsons then made a photostat copy of the Frasers' account and sent it with a covering letter to the Inspector of Police, East Sussex Constabulary, at Hailsham, the nearest town. A week later he received the following reply, dated 23 January 1962:

I have to inform you . . . that there is a 16th-century guest house named Walden Heath situated on the north side of the Lower Dicker to Herstmonceux road, A27, at Magham Down, Hailsham. As Mr and Mrs Fraser were travelling in a general direction from west to east this would, of course, have been on their left-hand side when they were proceeding to their hotel, The White Friars, Boreham Street. Walden Heath is situated about one and a half miles north-east of Hailsham and about four miles before reaching The White Friars.

Walden Heath is similar in appearance to the premises described by Mrs Fraser and is approximately fifteen yards from the A27 road and easily visible when passing. Suppers in addition to other meals are supplied at Walden Heath and the interior would, therefore, undoubtedly have been illuminated at 7.30 p.m., when lights would have been visible through the windows to motorists using the road.

It is also possible that when they returned later that evening after dinner Walden Heath had concluded business for that day and was in darkness. Although there are in fact unlighted signs at the edge of the road at Walden Heath premises giving the name and indicating that it is a 16th-century guest house, if such signs were missed the premises would give the appearance of a good-class country residence.

The following Sunday Mr Parsons and a friend journeyed to Sussex and had an excellent meal in the 'non-existent building'. It was 'Waldern-heath Fifteenth-Century Tea and Guest House', Amberstone Corner, Hailsham (not Walden Heath as in the police inspector's letter). Mr Parsons prepared a table which compared the items relating to the building in the Frasers' account with those he had observed personally. He concluded that it was remarkable that so little distortion or elaboration had accrued in the absence of a contemporary record. The only items which were wholly incorrect were those reporting a bar and bottles and a neon sign 'American bar'. 'Just as it was natural to assume that an ancient building was covered with lichen (as it was, though they could not have observed it), it was also natural to assume that a good hotel must have had a bar and bottles (which it had not), and in retrospect to give this assumption visual expression in the context of the memory.' The reason why the building could not be located on the return journey after 9 p.m. was that it was partly screened by trees and the lights in the two dining-rooms would have been switched off at 8 p.m., according to the proprietor.

Mr Parsons concluded:

> The acuity of the Frasers' observation is matched by their total failure to profit by it on subsequent occasions – failure to identify a building which turns out to be not only where they thought it was but which tallies with eighteen out of the twenty-one mental images they associated with it. We should indeed accord almost zero value to the type of statement with which accounts of such 'hallucination' cases always conclude: 'Although we searched everywhere and made all sorts of inquiries the building had vanished without trace.' The layman knows neither how to search nor how to make inquiries.

I am afraid I have to agree with the pessimistic statement in the last sentence. Requests to some of my correspondents to do something as simple as going to a certain address and establishing that it is a correct one and that someone of a certain name lives there often seem to baffle them. Although a careful search can result in a certain building being located, as we have seen in this chapter, it has been shown in the previous chapter that some buildings have been hallucinated and do not have, or never have had, a physical existence.

What is interesting about the two cases just quoted is that they show how people may have, in their minds, an image of an ideal scene and if any element is missing it is supplied in the recollection of that scene. Thus the tables set out for tea in the front garden of the house in Cornwall would have coloured umbrellas to provide shade for the residents, and there should be a bar to provide drinks for those dining at an attractive old guest house. In the first case the umbrellas at a café down the hill at Boscastle were transferred in memory to the house glimpsed by Mr and Mrs Pye, and in the second the neon sign 'American bar' was hallucinated by Mr and Mrs Fraser. It can also be argued that the Frasers hallucinated the lichen because in the darkness they could not have seen it although it did, as Mr Parsons has shown, exist.

Chapter 8

Sounds from the Sea

The 'adventure' of two Englishwomen, Mrs Dorothy Norton (pseudonym) and her sister-in-law Miss Agnes Norton (pseudonym), both in their early thirties, who while on holiday in France in August 1951 heard what was assumed to be a playback of the sounds of battle in the ill-fated Dieppe raid on 19 August 1942, during which Canadian forces suffered heavy casualties, was thought for a number of years to provide strong evidence for the reality of retrocognition. Indeed, Mrs Lucille Iremonger, who was highly critical of the earlier 'adventure' of Miss Moberly and Miss Jourdain in France, devoted a chapter to the Dieppe case in her book *The Ghosts of Versailles* by way of a rather grudging admission that there could be something in the concept of retrocognition. However, later research indicated that the sounds heard by the two women and interpreted by them as those made in a raid by Allied forces on a strongly fortified German position could have come from a dredger working nearby. However, was that the whole story? Let us first consider the evidence as set out by Mr G. W. Lambert and the Hon. Mrs Kathleen Gay in the May–June *Journal* of the SPR in 1952.

At the time of the 'adventure' Dorothy and Agnes Norton were staying at a house at Puys (Puits), which is 1½ miles east from Dieppe. They shared a bedroom on the second floor of a three-storey house facing the sea, which was about a quarter of a mile away, down a steep path. The house, they were informed, had been used as quarters for German troops during the war. Mrs Norton's two children and their nurse, who heard nothing unusual during the night, were in another bedroom on the same floor, two doors away. The time mentioned in the statements made afterwards to the SPR were taken from the women's wrist-watches which were set to a 'single summer time' (one hour ahead of GMT), which was also in use on 19 August 1942 for the Allied forces and also for civil purposes in France. Agnes Norton was in the Women's Royal Naval Service during the war and became accustomed to the accurate recording of time.

Dorothy Norton's statement about the events on Saturday 4 August 1951 is as follows:

> At 4.20 a.m. A. got up and went out of the room. I said 'Would you like to put the light on?' but she didn't. She came back in a few minutes. She said, 'Do you hear that noise?' I had in fact been listening to it for about twenty minutes. I woke up before it started. It started suddenly and sounded like a storm getting up at sea. A. said she had also been listening to it for about twenty minutes. We lay in the dark for a little listening to the sound. It sounded like a roar that ebbed and flowed, and we could distinctly hear the sound of cries and shouts and gunfire. We put the light on and it continued. We went out on the balcony where we could look down towards the beach, though we could not actually see the sea. The noise came from that direction and became very intense, it came in rolls of sound and the separate sounds of cries, guns and dive-bombing were very distinct. Many times we heard the sound of a shell at the same moment. The roaring became very loud. At 4.50 it suddenly stopped. At 5.05 a.m. it started again and once more became very intense, so much so that as we stood on our balcony, we were amazed that it did not wake other people in the house. By now it was getting light, cocks were crowing and birds were singing. We heard a rifle shot on the hill above the beach.
>
> The sounds became more distinctly those of dive-bombers rather than the cries and shouts we had heard earlier, although we could still hear them. The noise was very loud and came in waves as before. It stopped abruptly at 5.40.
>
> At 5.50 it started again but was not so loud and sounded like planes. This died away at 6 a.m. At 6.20 the sound became audible again but it was fainter than before, and I fell asleep as I was very tired.

Mrs Norton said she had been woken by a similar sound on Monday 30 July. It sounded exactly the same only fainter and not so intense. At the end she seemed to hear a lot of men singing. It ended when the cocks started crowing and she went to sleep. Her sister-in-law did not waken.

Miss Agnes Norton's statement of the happenings on Saturday 4 August followed:

> I woke in what I realized was very early morning although not yet dawn as no birds were singing. I was immediately aware of a most unusual series of sounds coming from the direction of the beach which were cries of men heard as if above a storm.
>
> After listening for about fifteen minutes I got up to leave the room and D. spoke to me and asked if I would like to put on the light which I did not in fact do. On my return I asked D. if she heard the noise too, and she said 'Yes', whereupon we put on the light and checked the time as 4.20 a.m. Our next move was out on to the balcony where the sounds intensified and appeared to me to be a mixture of gunfire, shellfire, dive-bombers, landing-craft and men's cries. All the sounds gave the impression of coming from a very long distance, i.e. like a broadcast from America in unmistakable waves of sound. At 4.50 a.m. all noise ceased abruptly and recommenced equally abruptly at 5.07 a.m. At 5.50 a.m. planes distinctly heard in large numbers and other fainter sounds dying away at 6 a.m. At 6.25 men's cries heard again growing gradually fainter and nothing at all heard after 6.55 a.m.

The statements were based on notes taken during the experience, which lasted nearly three hours, from 4 a.m. to 7 a.m. They were prepared partly on the same day (4 August) and partly on the following day, before the two ladies left for England. They were posted to the Society for Psychical Research by Mrs Norton with a covering letter dated 9 August, written after her return, describing the circumstances in which the experiences took place, and inquiring whether the society had had any other reports of this kind.

Commenting on the statements, Mr Lambert and Mrs Gay said that the remarkable feature of this case was the close correspondence between the times of the 'battle sounds' heard by the percipients on 4 August 1951 and the times of the actual battle sounds resulting from the operations on 19 August 1942, a correspondence which was brought out in tabular form in the *Journal* (see Table 1). The only account of the raid that was in the hands of the two women at the time was contained in a French guidebook entitled *Dieppe*. They had not read it before

Sounds from the Sea

Table 1 *Comparison between the experience of 4 August 1951 and the raid of 19 August 1942*

Percipients' Statements	Events on 19 August 1942
I. About 4 a.m. (i.e. about 20 minutes before 4.20). D. 'It [the noise] started suddenly and sounded like a storm getting up at sea . . . it sounded like a roar that ebbed and flowed . . . sounds of cries and shouts and gunfire.' A. '. . . unusual series of sounds coming from the direction of the beach which were cries of men heard as if above a storm.' Events on 19 August 1942	**3.47 a.m.** Assault vessels closing on Berneval ran across German convoy. Firing began immediately after, and went on until after 4 a.m. *Note.* This time (3.47 a.m.) was published in several accounts, e.g. *Combined Operations* (London: HMSO, 1943) and *The Green Beret* by Hilary St G. Saunders (London: Michael Joseph, 1949, p. 104). At Puys there was probably shouting by German soldiers manning the beach defences.
II 4.50 a.m. A. '. . . all noise ceased abruptly.' D. '. . . suddenly stopped.'	**4.50 a.m.** was zero hour for the flank landings, which, at Berneval and Puys, were delayed. There may have been silence at Puys at this stage. Several published reports mention 4.50 as zero hour but there is nothing to suggest that silence fell just then.
III. 5.07 a.m. A. '. . . recommenced abruptly at 5.07 a.m.' D. 'At 5.05 a.m. it started again and once more became very intense.'	**5.07 a.m.** The first wave of landing craft touched down at Puys in the face of heavy fire. *Note.* This time was published by inference in *The Canadian Army 1939–45.* The landing of the first wave is recorded as having been 17 minutes late – i.e. 4.50 plus 17 minutes.
	5.12 a.m. Destroyers started to bombard Dieppe.
D. 'The sounds became more distinctly that of dive-bombers rather than the cries and shouts we had heard earlier.'	**5.15 a.m.** Low-flying Hurricanes attacked the sea front buildings. **5.20 a.m.** The landing of the main force at Dieppe began, in the face of heavy fire.
IV. 5.40 a.m. D. 'It [the noise] stopped abruptly at 5.40.' (*Note.* A. does not mention this.)	**5.40 a.m.** The naval bombardment of Dieppe stopped. *Note.* A press correspondent in *The Times* of 21 August 1942, stated that the bombardment continued for 20 minutes after the landing had begun (i.e. till 5.20 plus 20 minutes).
V. 5.50 a.m. D. 'At 5.50 it started again . . . and sounded more like planes.'	**5.50 a.m.** Forty-eight RAF aircraft arrived from England. 'By now, shortly before 6 a.m . . . . the noise of aeroplanes had risen to a constant drone, like a net of harsh sound under the sky.' (Same correspondent as under IV above.)

Source Lambert and Gay, 1952: 614)

93

the experience started. After the noise had begun they read it on the balcony at about the middle of the third phase of the raid. The percipients' timetable could not have been obtained from the French acount, except perhaps the time 5.50 a.m. for the sound of aircraft at phase V. Both percipients were sure they they had never heard of the existence of any other reports, apart from the French guidebook and anything they may have read in the press at the time of the raid. Agnes Norton assured the investigators that during her service in the Women's Royal Naval Service she was not in a position to see unpublished naval reports of operations.

Table 1 indicates the correspondence between the sounds heard by the two Norton ladies and those during various episodes of the raid. The left-hand column divides the experience into phases I–V and under each phase brings together corresponding extracts from the statements of the two percipients. The right-hand column shows the officially recorded times of relevant events at the same hour of the day on 19 August 1942, and cites sources published before 4 August 1951.

Mr Lambert pointed out that as many supposed auditory hallu-cinations turned out on investigation to be cases in which some auditory noise had been misinterpreted, it was perhaps necessary to indicate that that explanation would not serve here. Any theory that the noises heard were due to water in pipes, or to artillery practice a long way off, the sound of which had been carried to Puys by some freak effect, would fail to explain why no one else heard the noises. The two women said that they had inquired during the day (4 August) of several persons whether they had been disturbed during the night by any unusual noises, and received negative answers. In particular, they asked a fellow visitor who had repeatedly complained of being disturbed at night by casual noises, as they had seen her bedroom light on when they were standing on the balcony listening to noises of 'amazing' loudness. She said she had not heard anything unusual. Nor could the noises have come from a cinema running through a film at an unusual hour, for there was no cinema in Puys.

On the other hand, it would, in our opinion, be rash to assume that the sounds heard were a sort of 'sound track' repetition of the sounds of the raid. The various kinds of sounds heard, gunfire, dive-bombing, planes, a rifle shot, shouts and cries, are all appropriate, but there is not enough detailed information available as to when the several kinds of sound first occurred to enable one to judge whether they are 'phased in' correctly.

(Lambert and Gay, 1952: 617)

Dorothy Norton had had three previous experiences of a 'psychic' nature, but none of them was a purely auditory hallucination, so she had no reason to expect an experience of that particular kind at Puys. Two of these earlier experiences were visual hallucinations which, though involving an apparition of a person well known to her, would not necessarily be considered evidential. The third took place one night during her visit to Dieppe at Easter. It, too, was not evidential. Consisting of a particularly powerful impression – possibly a dream – of someone being chased through her bedroom and towards the window, it was mainly of interest here because one might possibly associate it with events that took place during the raid of August 1942, though this did not seem to have occurred to the percipient. Agnes Norton had never had any other psychic experience, and it seemed likely that the presence of Dorothy Norton had something to do with her hearing hallucinatory sounds at all on 4 August.

The investigators conclude:

We have been impressed by the commendable pains taken by the percipients to record the evidence at once, on a day when they must have been busy preparing to return to England, and by the candour with which they have answered questions we have put to them. They both seemed to the investigators to be well-balanced individuals, with no tendency to add colour to their accounts. Neither of them has shown any concern whatever to 'prove' by the experience any preconceived theory of its cause, which would have been likely to determine the form it took. Both as regards form and content we think the experience must be rated a genuine psi phenomenon, of which little or nothing was derived from previous normally acquired knowledge.

(Lambert and Gay, 1952: 618)

But were the noises hallucinatory? This point was raised by Mr R. A. Eades, in a letter to the *Journal* for September 1968; he described how, towards the end of August 1951, he was returning with his family from a camping holiday in France and spent one night camping just outside Dieppe (to the east). 'During the night we were awakened by an indescribable noise which continued for several hours. Talking about it among ourselves we said it sounded like a zoo gone mad, like a fair, or like an amplified school playground, though, naturally, we did not think it was any of these things. The next morning I asked about this in the town and was told that it was the dredger which was then inactive in the harbour.'

Mr Eades added that his party also heard the sound in waves: 'this is normal when hearing distant sounds'. Although the noise was that of a loud sound far away, he said: 'I don't suppose the sound level was high where we were and it is not surprising that most people slept through it.' He had written to the Dieppe port authorities about the dredging service and was informed that the dredger operated from 00.15 hours to 08.15 hours on 4 August 1951.

Mr Lambert also consulted the harbour master at Dieppe, who furnished the times of working of the dredger there between 30 July and 5 August. On 30 July the dredger was worked between 10 and 11.30 a.m. and between 9.30 p.m. and midnight. On 4 August the hours of working were from fifteen minutes after midnight until 8.15 a.m. Mr Lambert said:

> It will be seen that on 30 July, when D. [Mrs Norton] alone heard faintly some strange noises, in the early morning 'before cockcrow', the dredger was not working; and on 4 August the dredger started about 3¾ hours before the 'battle noises', and stopped about 1¼ hours after the 'battle noises' had stopped. Quite apart from the difference in the character in the two sets of noises, I find it hard to believe that the dredger, even if it had been only subconsciously heard, could have acted as a subliminal stimulus to cause the experience.

> (ibid.: 358)

Mr Robert J. Hastings, a pertinacious investigator, now joined in the controversy. In a paper in the *Journal* for June 1969 he made the interesting point that in one important respect the Dieppe Raid case stood as an 'odd man out' among all other cases of paranormal visual or auditory experiences associated with particular places. In other well-authenticated cases with which he was acquainted, including the Versailles case, the percipients had not realized *at the time of the experience* that what they were seeing or hearing was paranormal, whereas in the Dieppe Raid case, which lasted about three hours, the percipients were in a sufficiently normal state to be critical of their experience during the whole of that time. He suggested that real aircraft might have been responsible for the sound of aircraft reported by the two ladies, as Puys lies in the path of aircraft flying from London to Paris. He also suggested that much of what the ladies heard might be attributable to the sound of the sea, distorted perhaps by the surrounding cliffs which were generally about 250 feet high.

Mr Hastings considered that by itself the sound of the dredger might not be quite a perfect explanation for what occurred, for the times it was known to have been working did not correspond exactly to the times mentioned in the percipients' statements; but the sound of the dredger coming from a distance, together with the sound of the sea nearby, distorted perhaps by acoustic effects due to the conformation of the cliffs, might well have produced a pandemonium which visitors to Puys could be forgiven for failing to identify. Also, evidence that the ladies were acquainted with the sounds that were normal at night at Puys, which was needed as a basis for comparison before paranormality could be postulated, was missing.

Answering the arguments about aircraft, Mr Lambert pointed out that, according to the official report, there was no air activity at Puys. Just before the landing-craft touched down there was no doubt a heavy sound of RAF planes attacking Dieppe, which was being prepared for the main landing, but the plan required the RAF to keep clear of the beaches selected for the flank landings, where it was hoped to get ashore by surprise. Both percipients had had war service and must be assumed to be well able to distinguish between the occasional sound of civil aircraft passing steadily overhead on a recognized route, and the sound of RAF planes flying in mass formation and dive-bombing at their objectives. 'If the whole experience was due to ordinary noises heard in an unfamiliar environment', Mr Lambert argued, 'and some of them were described as "very loud", why did no one else hear them?'

Dr Michael Coleman joined the debate in his book *The Ghosts of the Trianons*. He believed that there was a natural explanation for the noises heard by the two ladies – the working of the dredger – and said that 'Lambert sought to refute this explanation by pointing out that on the day in question the dredger started nearly four hours before the Nortons heard the "battle noises" and continued for more than an hour after the noises ceased. (Since neither of the ladies woke before 4 a.m., however, the "early start" is readily explained, and a change in wind direction – or even town noises, starting at 7 a.m. – could explain the "late finish".)'.

My reaction to this is to point out that Mrs Norton was awake before the noise started and 'it started suddenly and sounded like a storm getting up at sea'. If the noise she heard was that caused by the dredger surely that would have registered with her on waking. I do not think that you can argue that a change in wind direction could have resulted in the noise of the dredger not being heard after 6 a.m. when the dredger was, in fact, still working, without advancing evidence to prove this contention. Also, I do not think we can assume that 'town noises' would approximate to those made by a dredger working.

When we analyse this case we have to bear in mind that what explanation we accept will depend on the interpretation we make of sounds coming from the direction of the sea at a particular time and in a particular place. The sounds heard by Mrs Norton and Miss Norton were at Puys, which was in the battle zone (a German howitzer was in action a few hundred yards south of Puys, firing overhead at Allied shipping lying off the shore, and landing-craft touched down at Puys). The sounds heard by Mrs Norton were of 'cries, guns and dive-bombing' and were 'very distinct'. Those heard by Miss Norton appeared to her to be 'a mixture of gunfire, shellfire, dive-bombers, landing-craft and men's cries'. Mr Eades and his family were camped 'just outside Dieppe to the east', which would also be in the battle zone. His description of the sounds his party heard differs greatly from those given by the two Norton ladies. The sounds heard by the Eades party were like those of 'a zoo gone mad, like a fair, or like an amplified school playground'. There is nothing here to suggest that the noises heard could be compared with those made by a Combined Operations raid on the coast. We also have to bear in mind that the Eades party was almost certainly camped closer to the origin of the sounds made by the dredger than the two Norton ladies at Puys, 1½ miles away. Also, if the sounds heard by the Eades party towards the end of August had been heard by them on 4 August, the date of the Nortons' experience, a valid comparison could be made, making due allowance for the distances involved, but not otherwise.

Some puzzling facts remain. During the day, following their unusual experience, the two Norton ladies asked several persons whether they had been disturbed during the night by any unusual noise 'and received negative answers'. In particular they asked a fellow visitor who had repeatedly complained of being disturbed at night by casual noises whether she had been disturbed; they knew that she was awake while they were standing on the balcony listening to noises of 'amazing' loudness as they had seen her bedroom light on, but she replied that she had not heard anything unusual. What are we to make of that? Had the fellow guest, and the others questioned, heard the dredger at work and taken the noise it made for granted, or did the noise not carry as far as Puys? We do not know. Because of this uncertainty we have to suspend judgement on this case, but I do not assume we can take it for granted that it has been 'explained away' because a dredger was working in Dieppe harbour on the night Mrs Norton and Miss Norton had their 'adventure'.

Chapter 9

Figures in a Landscape

In the previous chapter only the sounds of a battle in the past were heard, if we exclude the possible explanation that they were made by a dredger at work at the time of the experience. However, other experiences connected with battles in the past are characterized by the sight of large numbers of men moving noiselessly. Two accounts are given in this chapter, the first involving one percipient, the second, two. The first account, 'A vision of the aftermath of the battle of Nechtanesmere AD 685', by Dr James F. McHarg, first published in the *Journal* of the SPR for December 1978, has already been given a good deal of publicity, but I am summarizing it again to bring out certain evidential details which, in my opinion, have received insufficient attention. In his introduction to the case, Dr McHarg, a retired consultant psychiatrist, of Dundee, said: 'In recording this experience, no *evidential* significance is implied. it was merely thought desirable to record the incident, despite the interval of time since its occurrence, before the experient became too old – and without regard to possible explanations for the apparition,' Despite this disclaimer, I believe there are evidential aspects to the case.

But first of all, the battle of Nectanesmere: this was generally regarded, in the late seventh century AD, as one of the outstanding events of the age. It took place on the afternoon of Saturday 20 May 685, and in it the Northumbrians under their King, Ecgfrith, were decisively beaten by the Picts, under their King, Brude mac Beli. The battle marked the end of an aggressive expedition by Ecgfrith, undertaken against the advice of St Cuthbert and other Northumbrians. Little is known for certain about the expedition prior to the battle, but it has been suggested that the Northumbrians, already in control in the Lothians, crossed the Forth near Stirling and the Tay near Perth. Of the two alternative routes after that – south or north of the Sidlaw Hills

– it is thought more probable that they took the northern route through Strathmore as far as Dunnichen Hill. The suggestion is that Ecgfrith was there drawn off his route by a feigned Pictish retreat through the cleft in that hill and that the Northumbrians, bursting through the cleft, realized too late that the Pictish fortress on the south side, invisible from the north, lay only 300–400 yards to their left. It is presumed that the Picts, with reinforcements from the fortress, quickly turned the retreat by the Northumbrians into a flight downhill towards the mere at the bottom, Ecgfrith himself was slain and his whole royal bodyguard around him. Most of the Northumbrian army was killed – the few who survived, no doubt, saving themselves by flight. Ecgfrith's body was carried off to the royal burial ground at Iona. The activity of dealing with the dead after the battle, presumably by the Picts themselves, would no doubt have continued throughout the following night.

The percipient in this case was Miss E. F. Smith, of Letham, Angus, then in her late fifties, who on 2 January 1950 attended a cocktail party at a friend's house at Brechin, 10 miles to the north of Letham, and stayed on for dinner. A fall of snow had been followed by rain and, 2 miles outside Brechin, the car skidded into a ditch. There was no question of the skid being due to her fainting, or any other lapse of consciousness, nor of Miss Smith having been injured in any way, or concussed. She had to abandon her car, however, and continue her journey on foot, a distance of about 8 miles. Her walk was along deserted country roads in a countryside with a few scattered farms. She had her little dog with her but, for the last 2 miles of the journey, she had to carry him on her shoulder, and, as she neared Letham, she must have felt fairly exhausted. She had also felt 'nervous' immediately prior to the onset of the apparitional experience for she had deliberately refrained from taking a commonly used, and normally welcome, short-cut because it would have taken her out of the open country and alongside a dark, wooded area.

The apparitional experience began when Miss Smith was about half a mile from the first houses of Letham village and it continued until she reached them. The time was getting on for 2 a.m. The first phase started as Miss Smith approached a crest of the road over which, by daylight, the top of Dunnichen Hill would first have come into sight, and then its base, straight ahead of her, about a mile away, at which she first saw moving torches.

Continuing her journey Miss Smith made, at a T-junction, a turn to the left towards Letham so that the distant lights were on her right. The second phase of the experience began a little lower down the winding road as she watched, on her right, in the middle distance, about a third of a mile away, further figures carrying torches. The third phase followed quickly upon this as the watched figures were even closer to her, in the field on the right, about 50 yards away in the direction of some farm buildings, which were not, however, visible in the darkness.

At this stage the dog began to growl. Miss Smith said, 'He was sitting on my left shoulder and turned and looked at the lights and started growling and I thought "now next he's going to bark."' She was anxious that the dog should not bark and wake up the village. The experience, which lasted, Dr McHarg estimated, about twelve minutes, ended when Miss Smith left the scene with the figures and torches behind her as she entered the village through which she continued her walk to her own home – a distance of perhaps a further quarter of a mile, after which she went straight to bed.

'It had been an exclusively visual experience', said Dr McHarg. 'There had been no preceding auditory or olfactory experience to suggest a temporal lobe disturbance. Only on waking in the morning, she said, had she realized what a strange experience it had been.'

Miss Smith was not interviewed until 22 September 1971, twenty-one years after her experience. She was then in her seventies and has since died. Dr McHarg arrived at her house with Malcolm McFadyen, clinical psychologist, and Alec Bell, technician, who supervised the tape-recording to which Miss Smith had agreed. After the initial recording the team took Miss Smith slowly, in a car, over the route she had been walking during the experience, and she pointed out, from different points along the road, the sites and distances of the successive components of the apparitional happenings. Then they returned to Miss Smith's house and recorded some further, clarifying discussion.

The mere or loch, the site of the battle, no longer exists, and, indeed, its original site was long a matter of conjecture. A patchwork of fields, with their fences and boundaries, effectively camouflages it, and, as viewed from the surrounding roads, there is at present nothing to indicate its original outline or even to suggest a loch had ever been there. The late Dr F. T. Wainwright, one-time head of the Department of History at Queen's College, Dundee, had noticed, in 1947, how floods following the winter of 1946–47 had temporarily restored at least part of the old loch and how, in the following summer, as a result of faint colour changes in the growing grasses, the flood marks in the fields could still be seen. Dr Wainwright determined to try to indicate on a map the extent of the vanished loch and this he did with the aid of photography and a field survey to determine contour lines. The map showed, in particular, a finger of the loch projecting in a north-easterly direction, round which people moving towards the east would have had to skirt.

Asked about her experience, Miss Smith said that at the beginning of the first phase, in the distance straight ahead, she saw 'people who looked as if they were carrying flaming torches . . . and there were quite a lot of torches'. Miss Smith felt that what she was seeing had not suddenly started but that it had been already going on when she came upon it. Her recalled reaction was to say to herself, 'Well, that's an incredible thing.' The nearer figures carrying torches, which she saw during the second phase, were, she said, 'quite obviously skirting the mere, because they didn't walk, from where I was looking, straight across to the far corner of the field, they *came round*'. Speaking about the nearest figures of all, which she watched during the third phase, Miss Smith said, 'They were obviously looking for their own dead . . . the one I was watching, the one nearest the roadside, would bend down and turn a body over and, if he didn't like the look of it, he just turned it back on its face and went over to the next one . . . . There were several of them . . . . I *supposed* they were going to bury them.'

When asked about clothing Miss Smith said: 'They looked as if they were in – well, I would have said brown, but that was merely the light – anyway, dark tights, the whole way up . . . a sort of overall, with a roll-collar, and at the end of their tunics there was a larger roll round them too. And it simply went on looking like tights until it reached their feet. I did not see what was on their feet. But there weren't long boots.' A tracing from a photograph of an incised figure of a Pictish warrior on a stone at Golspie shows a bootless figure; it gives the impression of tights, and also of a roll-necked tunic with what could be a 'roll' at the bottom of it.

When asked specifically about headgear, Miss Smith said that the figures she saw were wearing 'the kind of thing a baker's boy use to wear . . . . Just like a hard roll, round, stuck on the top of their heads . . . excellent for carrying things on the top of the head with.'

Miss Smith was asked about the torches the figures she saw were carrying. She replied: 'They were carrying very long torches in their left hands . . . [the torches were] *very* red . . . . Afterwards', she continued, 'I wondered what they were made of – tar, I suppose. *Was* there tar in those days?' At the time of the interview Dr McHarg assumed that Miss Smith meant that it had been the flames of the torches which had been unusually red, but she may equally well have meant that it had been their shafts. Inquiries revealed that torches in Scotland used to be made from the resinous roots of the Scots fir which, in their natural state, do indeed have a distinctive red colour; such roots would have been available at Nechtanesmere, for Dunnichen Hill was crowned then, no doubt, as it is today, with the Scots fir of the old Caledonian Forest.

Dr McHarg remarked: 'If all this is so, Miss Smith's surprise at the redness of the torches may be a point of significance because her supposition that they were made of tar clearly indicates that there had not been any preconceived idea, at the back of her own mind, that the torches would have been made of the roots of the Scots fir and, therefore, "very long", and red in colour.'

In his assessment of the case, Dr McHarg suggested that there seemed to be three basic possibilities. First, that there had been no apparition at all, and that the whole thing had been a fraud or a hoax; second, that there had been no apparitional experience, but that, without any question of a hoax, a false memory arose in Miss Smith's mind on the following morning, based upon mere musings she had had the previous night while passing the site of the ancient battle; and third, that she did have the series of visual experiences essentially as she had described it.

If the apparitional experience really did occur as described, it seemed probable to Dr McHarg that Miss Smith had been in 'an altered state of consciousness' at the time, as suggested by the temporary suspension of her full reflective and critical faculties, which made her, strangely, more concerned about her dog waking the village than about the apparent fact that she was witnessing an event from so long ago. 'The cause of such an alteration in consciousness might have been related to exhaustion and cold and perhaps to the apprehension, at the start of the experience, which, she remembered, had prevented her from taking an otherwise tempting short-cut near the end of her long and tiring walk.'

Posing the question of how the 'elaborate content' of the experience could be explained, Dr McHarg asked if it could be based upon cryptomnesic (hidden) knowledge acquired by a forgotten reading of a paper by Dr Wainwright in 1948 in the journal *Antiquity* on the site of the battle of Nechtanesmere, or by a forgotten hearing of discussion about his findings or the survey work upon which they had been based. Miss Smith replied that she had heard about the battle of Nechtanesmere but had not known who were the contestants. She also said she had heard of Dr Wainwright, but had not met him before the experience, although she had met him afterwards. Reminded by Dr McHarg that Dr Wainwright had published his paper just two years before her experience, and asked if she had any recollection of having seen, or heard of, the paper beforehand, Miss Smith answered: 'I had not *seen* it before I saw this. Someone gave it to me, after, to read, but I merely told him I was one up on him!'

Dr McHarg was impressed by the apparently correct locating by Miss Smith of the gently undulating landscape of the tip of the north-easterly finger of the mere – i.e. the point round which the moving figures, skirting the edge of the mere, seemed to move as they came towards 'the far corner of the field'. His opinion was that it would have required a practised map-reader, which Miss Smith certainly was not, to have transferred Dr Wainwright's mapped information so precisely and so correctly on to the landscape as viewed from the part of the road where she was.

Dr McHarg considered that certain features of the apparition appear not to be related to explicit features of Dr Wainwright's work and paper – e.g. the extension so far east of the searching (presumably by the Picts) for their dead; the details of clothing and, in particular, of the curious headgear; and the redness of the torches. Miss Smith did *not* report that she saw the 'head-rings' being utilized for the transport of the bodies, by Picts working in pairs. 'It is surely possible, however, that the ancient Picts, like present-day Africans, were in the habit of carrying burdens on their heads, and of wearing a hard ring on the head for this purpose. That corpses might have been carried in this way would seem to be the sort of detail which might conceivably receive future verification as a result of increased knowledge about Pictish practices.'

I asked Dr McHarg if he thought Miss Smith's attendance at a cocktail party the previous evening should be taken into consideration. he replied that he did not think this was relevant, as Miss Smith had stayed for dinner after the party and had left Brechin after midnight. She herself had said, laughingly, that her friends naturally told her she must have had too much to drink, but she had not. In any case, Dr McHarg pointed out, an 8-mile walk would have sobered her up! 'But, more important, the idea that alcoholic *intoxication* (drunkenness) causes hallucinations is a fallacy – popular notion though it be. The notion is based, no doubt, on the visual hallucinations which do accompany alcoholic *delirium* (delirium tremens), which is a very different matter, and a disabling physical illness lasting several days.'

Dr McHarg agreed with me that the alcohol might have lowered 'the barriers of inhibition' in Miss Smith, adding: 'At the time of interviewing Miss Smith I had not suspected any current misuse of alcohol – but it was impossible to know, in retrospect, what part it *might* have played all those years ago. One thing one could be sure of would be that alcohol could not explain the specific *content* of the visual experiences.'

One conclusion that occurred to me later was that as Miss Smith saw the figures with torches moving round the edges of what had once been a loch, or lake, whereas it was now solid ground, the scenery of the past had been substituted for that of the present. A key phrase in the *Journal* report, referring to Miss Smith's experience (phase three) was that she watched figures even closer to her than before, in the field on the right, about 50 yards away in the direction of some farm buildings – which, however, were not visible in the darkness. I maintain that these buildings should have been visible in the light of the torches being carried by the searching figures. The reason they were not visible was not because of the darkness but because another landscape had been substituted for the one that contained them.

I raised with Dr McHarg some questions about this case in the late summer of 1990. Answering them, he wrote, 'Thinking again about the whole case, I find it difficult to exclude the possibility of Wainwright's work, not so long before the experience, playing a significant part. I have already mentioned difficulties about a "normal", cryptomnesic, part played by Wainwright's work. A paranormal part continues, however, as a possibility, such as telepathic contact with Wainwright or some other archaeologically knowledgeable person.'

This raises an interesting point (about super ESP), which I will discuss in the Appendix.

The other case concerning moving figures with torches comes from Joan Forman's book *The Mask of Time* (1978). Mrs Sheila White, a doctor's widow on the Isle of Wight, told how on 4 January 1969 she and her late husband were on their way by car to dine with friends at Niton and decided to take the leisurely road across the downs of the island. The night was dark with towering cloud masses, but above them a brilliant full moon sharply etched the scene in black, grey and silver. They began to climb the first hill approaching the downs, with chalk pits on the left and fields to the right of the road. This was a lonely area, with the nearest farmhouse some miles away, and the last thing the travellers expected at this point was what they saw before them. The fields appeared to be covered with bobbing lights, as though many people were moving about there. The couple were surprised but attributed the sight to shepherds busy at work among their sheep, since it was the time of the year for lambing.

The doctor and his wife topped the hill and were about to drive down it when they noticed that all the fields to their right also were ablaze with lights – 'like a great city'. They stopped the car and gazed astonished at the myriad twinkling points, trying to decide what they were seeing. It apparently did not occur to them that the explanation was not a rational one. They assumed they must be looking at some kind of agricultural exhibition, though early January was hardly the time for such an activity in open country. In the distance what they remembered as a simple cart track to an outlying farm seemed now to be a well-lit city street, with buildings on either side; the lights were of green, red and orange. The effect of these experiences was disorientating. The feeling of unreality was heightened when they arrived at the farm track to find that it was its usual deserted self, dark with shadow and blanched with moonlight, but without building or artificial light of any kind along its length.

The couple were by now unnerved. Mrs White in particular looked forward to reaching a familiar landmark: an island inn, the Hare and Hounds, a squat, friendly dwelling at the crossroads to

Newport on the one hand and Merstone on the other. They turned the corner and there certainly was the inn, but it was bathed in light and surrounded by what appeared to be figures carrying torches who ran backwards and forwards across the road ahead. One figure stood out from the rest: an exceptionally tall man with clear-cut features who ran directly in front of the car. He wore a leather jerkin with a broad belt. The fields were brightly lit, and the wash of light appeared to continue some distance towards Newport, fields and hedges lost in it.

At this stage Dr White, a very logical person according to his wife, decided that some questions needed answers and determined to stop and ask one of the people ahead what was the cause of so much activity and illumination. When the car was about 20 yards from the Hare and Hounds both lights and figures disappeared, vanishing as though a switch had been thrown. The pub was in darkness save for the usual small illumination from its windows. The unnerved couple drove on, without stopping, until they reached their destination.

They returned that way in the early hours of the morning and the landscape had reverted to normal, the feeling of oppressiveness had dispersed, the sense of unreality dissipated. The towering clouds had also gone and the moon rode free in a clear sky.

Afterwards the Whites sought explanations. Were they the witnesses of a mirage caused by a reflected or refracted image of a nearby city thrown against the cloud barriers and thence to the fields beneath? Only the waters of the Solent separate the city of Portsmouth from the Isle of Wight. An interesting thought, said the author, but not, she thought, a viable one, for it failed to explain the figures with torches, or the man in the leather jerkin passing in front of the car.

Mrs White suggested to the author that the strange experience showed either a past or future sequence of life in that area and Miss Forman agreed with her:

> The Roman legions once camped and marched across Vectis (the name they gave to the island). Roman camps were built with at least two streets intersecting at right angles in the case of temporary structures; and on a complete grid-system where a permanent fort was intended (the legionary fortress of Caerleon is a good example). Torches were certainly used for

108

lighting purposes throughout the empire, and one would expect to find a camp adequately lit, especially in time of peace. A past sequence is therefore a strong possibility in this case. Vectis was later occupied by the invading Vikings, who set up winter camps there in the late tenth century and used the island as a base from which to attack the mainland. The type of dress worn by the Whites' tall apparition conforms more nearly to Viking than Roman costume. The Norsemen were a tall race.

(1978: 56)

I feel that the details of the tall man's dress given by Mrs White – a leather jerkin with a broad belt – are insufficient for purposes of identification of the race of the wearer. Bede states that the island was occupied by Jutes after Roman domination ended, but according to the Anglo-Saxon *Chronicle* Cerdic, of the West Saxons, seized the island in AD 530 after a fight at Carisbrooke. Also, from the fourteenth century to the sixteenth the French made frequent descents upon the island.

It seems that Dr and Mrs White saw figures from some unspecified period in the past moving in a hallucinated landscape, vividly lit, but not one which substituted the landscape of the present for one of the past. The proof of this is that a familiar landmark, the Hare and Hounds pub, was seen by them. Their arrival at the pub marked a return to everyday reality for they were plunged into the darkness of the downs and the figures with torches disappeared with the lights that illuminated them.

Chapter 10

A Dangerous Walk
on the Cliffs

A case of apparent retrocognition in 1938 in which a man came close to serious injury, or even death, when he narrowly averted a fall from a cliff in a Devonshire cove because he hallucinated features of the landscape, has been the subject of controversy ever since. A natural explanation of what took place was advanced after the report of the incident was first published in the June–July issue of the SPR *Journal* in 1947, but did this supply the complete answer? I have reservations because the sensations during the experiences described by Mr J. S. Spence, who supplied the account, have much in common with those of the participants in the Versailles and Kersey cases.

The case was sent to the society by Mr Spence in 1940 but owing to war conditions was not followed up at the time. Mr Spence was interviewed by the society's research officer on 29 May 1947 and explained that his memory of what had taken place had become too hazy for him to give further details, as he could have done when he sent the account. When the experience occurred he had not read *An Adventure*; on doing so eighteen months later he thought it worth reporting his own case as being of an apparently similar type.

Mr Spence's statement is as follows:

> On an unusually warm, sunny morning in March 1938 I walked down to a Devonshire cove, which impressed and elated me by its tranquillity after the rush and noise of London. I strolled casually across the beach, exploring the rocks and pools, towards the end of the headland on the far side. As I went the atmosphere, which had at first so much appealed, grew heavy and depressing. Eventually, in a little inlet in the headland, I came

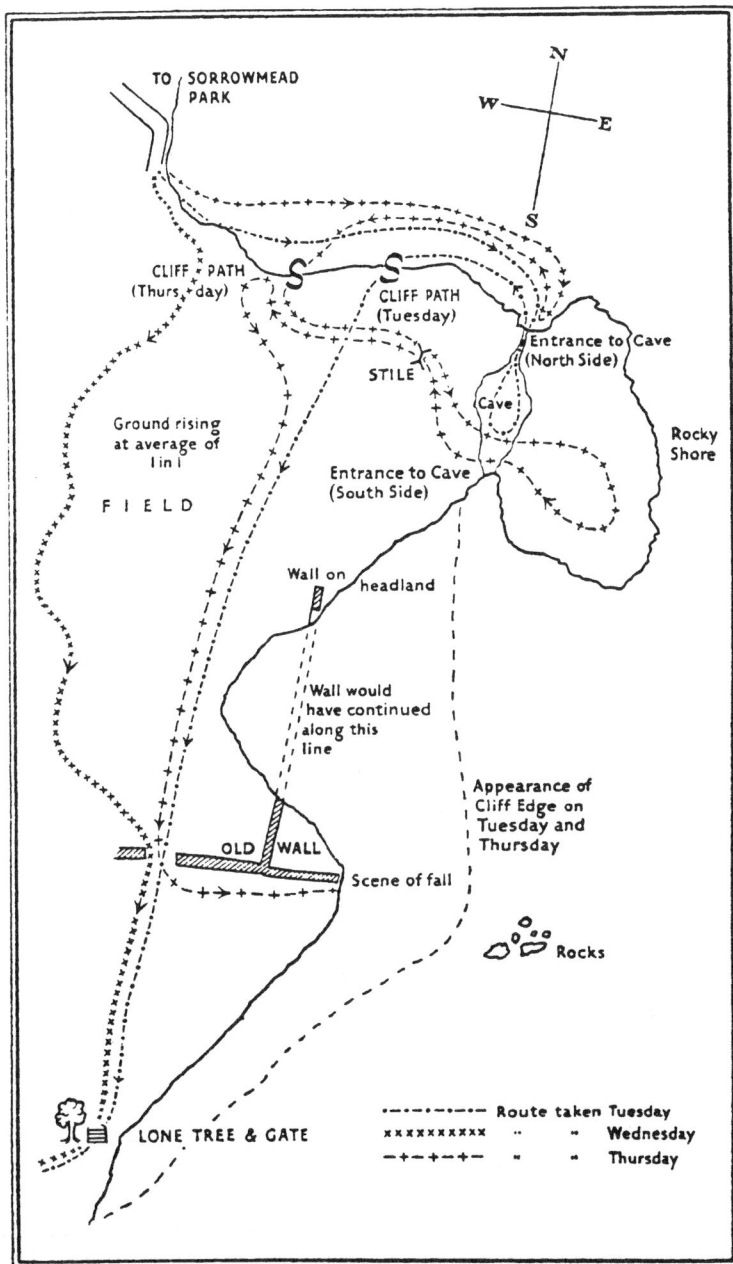

TO SORROWMEAD PARK

N
W
E
S

CLIFF PATH
(Thursday)

CLIFF PATH
(Tuesday)

STILE

Entrance to Cave
(North Side)

Cave

Ground rising
at average of
1 in 1

FIELD

Entrance to Cave
(South Side)

Rocky
Shore

Wall on   headland

Wall would
have continued
along this
line

Appearance of
Cliff Edge on
Tuesday and
Thursday

OLD WALL

Scene of fall

Rocks

LONE TREE & GATE

----·----·----	Route taken Tuesday
xxxxxxxxx	" " Wednesday
-+-+-+-	" " Thursday

upon a cave which seemed large enough to enter on hands and knees. I felt very much afraid but curiosity drove me into it. A few yards down the tunnel I noticed daylight ahead and after a further two or three yards I found myself in a vast cave which apparently extended to the further side of the headland as I was only in semi-darkness.

Although there was clearly no one in the cave I had an unpleasant feeling of being watched and scrambled back to the cove through the little tunnel as quickly as was consistent with self-respect. I now sought and found a little path by which I could clamber up the cliff, and once on top I set out to climb to the summit of the ridge, less than a quarter of a mile away. I now felt even more depressed and lonely than before and had the impression that something was straining at a leash so that one could almost hear the noise that something made, trying to break the bonds. However, I went on slowly, though waist-deep in bracken and bramble. After ten minutes or so I came upon a long old-fashioned type of wall made of slabs of stone and earth – no mortar. The stone looked very fresh and there were no creepers on it. As I passed through a gap, left as if for a gate, I noticed that the wall stretched about 80 yards or so over grass, bramble and bracken to the edge of the cliff, which was there very high. Almost at right angles to it another wall sloped steeply down the hill and disappeared among the scrub and bracken on the headland.

I was puzzled why the walls should be there but decided that if I were not to be late for lunch I must hurry on to my objective, a point where, according to a large-scale Ordnance map, I would find a solitary tree beside an old gate. On looking ahead I saw neither the tree nor the gate, but a mass of stunted trees, bent by the prevailing wind. The heat was terrific and the stillness awful so I hurried on to get into the shade. As I went forward the atmosphere became less charged and less tense and for the first time since I had entered the cove about half an hour earlier, I heard a definitely real sound: a seagull flew over my head screaming. Then, to my surprise, I saw ahead the lone tree and gate and I was also surprised to find on looking back that the grass seemed greener and fresher and the bracken less than when I had passed through it. The wall was apparently hidden behind the brow of the hill. My head was aching less and I could breathe more easily. When I got home I felt astonishingly weary and my usual good appetite had quite disappeared.

The next day I decided to set forth on the same walk about the same time. The sun was even warmer than the day before but the odd depressing feeling and the strange stillness had gone. On reaching the cove I was surprised to find the tide right up, for the day before it must have been low to enable me to cross the beach to the cave in the headland. Surely, I thought, the tide cannot alter more than an hour a day. I turned back and climbed the hill behind towards the summit of the ridge and the wall. On reaching the top I was amazed to find myself near the edge of a cliff, and with no sign of a long new wall, and I thought I must have gone wrong. There was certainly a very old scrap of wall covered in ivy, with another portion leaving it at right angles, but within a few feet it broke off at the end of a cliff. My eye then followed the branch wall, expecting to see it disappear in scrub, but it, too, stopped abruptly, very dilapidated, at the edge of the cliff.

For a while this puzzled me: then I gave it up and walked on. Almost at once I was startled to see the lone tree and the gate. I was certain I had been in the same spot the day before and had seen only a mass of bent and stunted trees and I knew I had seen a long new wall. I came to the conclusion I must have taken the wrong path and I decided to return the next day with a torch and a camera and explore the cave and find the wall. How I had come to miss my way in such a small area was beyond me.

I reached the cove next morning to find the tide fairly full and I could not get across to the cave for a couple of hours. I distinctly remembered the little inlet in the headland where I had entered the cave at sea level but on reaching it there was no cave. I at last found, a few feet up in a pile of shale and hidden by a large boulder, an entrance to what was obviously a cave, but far smaller than it had been two days before. As a large pile of shale showed signs of collapse and there was hardly room to wriggle in, I decided not to risk it and walked back to find the path by which I had climbed the cliff. This was not to be seen, but further along I found another which led up to the headland. Here, to satisfy myself as to my whereabouts, I made my way through some bracken and over a stile to the end of the headland and then returned to where I expected to find the top of the path by which I had climbed the first day. The place, however, looked impossible to get down and I wondered how I had ever got up, so I decided to go along the cliff towards Dartmouth. As I reached the top of the cliff path the atmosphere became charged and unfriendly again. I had the same tight feeling across my forehead and felt the same sweat breaking out.

There came that peculiar sensation of something straining at its leash. There was no particular sound to this effect, to which I could have stopped and listened, and possibly logically explained, but I received the impression, on a much larger scale, as it were, of a cart-horse straining at a wagon-load of bricks which it could not possibly drag.

I moved on mechanically through the ferns, which suddenly seemed to have become waist-deep again, and it was with considerable difficulty that I made any progress.

I had forgotten about the wall until I came to it, in front of me with its new-looking slabs of stone, neatly placed into and against each other. Down to the left it stretched for some way, over grass and brambles and bracken to the edge of the cliff. Furthermore, another wall jutted away from it almost at right angles, and sloped sharply down the hill, nearly in the direction in which I had come, and disappeared amongst scrubs and undergrowth somewhere on the headland.

I went up close to the wall and walked a few paces forward. I felt giddy, as if looking from a great height, but in front of me, without any doubt stretched the wall. On an impulse, I pulled out my camera, and attempted to find an object in the view-finder, but my giddiness increased and I clicked the shutter with very little care. I put the camera away in my pocket and prepared to move forward.

I had gone only one short pace, when I felt my left foot slip, and go down as if in a rabbit hole. The shock threw me off my balance, and my left foot twisted so that I felt my body collapse. As I fell, my hand grasped wildly and came into contact with tufts of think coarse grass, and I held on tight. My body came to rest on my twisted left foot, while my right shot into space. For a few moments everything went black.

When I opened my eyes I immediately became aware of two things: the shrieking of the seagulls, and the very dangerous position in which I was. Two small sturdy tufts of grass, and

114

a ledge a few inches wide, on which my left foot lay, had saved me from the rocks below. Almost immediately above my head was the broken fragment of an old ivy-covered wall.

For some minutes I clung to the grass and dared not move. When some composure returned, I realized the seriousness of the position. With great care I gradually wormed my way to a cautious standing position, though the whole of my weight, until I could bring my right foot on to the ledge, had to be thrown on to the damaged left. Then I caught hold of a large tuft of grass further away from the edge of the cliff, tested it, and pulled my right leg up and on to the top of the cliff. The left leg followed slowly. I dared not look back, but carefully I manoeuvred my way on my stomach to a safe position some yards from the top of the cliff.

After a few minutes my mind cleared a little. The atmosphere had returned to normal, and the tremendous pressure that I had felt had gone. I looked to the right. The lone tree and gate were in their proper positions. Out in front, were the wall had stretched, was nothing but space, but some distance out at sea there was a group of rocks.

Then, as if suddenly becoming aware of my recent escape, I got up and as quickly as possible set off home. Down the slope towards the cove I suddenly remembered the portion of the wall that had jutted out at right angles, which had appeared to stretch to the headland, to be lost in brambles. So I went out to the headland and after a long search found not far from the edge of the cliff and directly in line with the tumbledown bit, which could be seen on top of the ridge, a fragment of wall, buried in the bramble [a photograph of this section of wall taken after the experience and one taken by Mr Spence just before he nearly walked off the cliff edge accompanied his article in the *Journal*].

Mr Spence added some comments.
He visited the cove on three consecutive days; Tuesday, Wednesday and Thursday. The atmosphere on the Wednesday was normal, and different from the Tuesday visit and the latter part of Thursday's. 'If I got some glimpse of this corner of the world as it was, possibly centuries ago, I must have been under that spell only for certain definite periods.'
On the Tuesday he felt the oppression as soon as he reached the

beach, and throughout the period in question, until a short while after the left the ridge and saw the solitary tree and gate, which had appeared as a mass of stunted trees when he had viewed it from the vicinity of the wall.

The Wednesday was a perfectly normal time, although the weather and temperature remained the same.

On the Thursday everything was normal until the moment when he turned from the cliff path because he did not think he could get down. There was little doubt that the path had disappeared. Instead of a field he found waist-deep bracken. 'Conditions in the atmosphere became worse as I reached the summit, where the pressure was terrific.'

The tide could not be explained reasonably. On the Tuesday the tide was right out, a distance of at least 150 yards, and on the Wednesday and Thursday practically full. As it was the same time every day this was, according to the law of the tides, impossible.

Mr Spence considered that the cave must have some connection with the rest of the experience. On the Tuesday the cave was easily found, but not on the Thursday when it appeared that a landslide had occurred.

The path altered its situation.

Between the cove and the wall the field was normally covered in grass and primroses in March but on the Tuesday and Thursday it was thick bracken.

The lone tree and gate seemed to appear and disappear quite casually. On the Tuesday, from the wall, Mr Spence saw only stunted trees. Yet he had to go only a short distance before the vision cleared and he saw the tree and gate a little way off. He noted too, on looking back, that the ground looked less withered.

The subject of the wall was the most interesting 'because of its weird persistence in being so out of place, and because of its perfect transfiguration'. Although, on the Thursday, he thought the old portion lay at the end of the new stretch, he could not see if this was so because of the brambles.

Mr Spence thought that his giddiness was obviously due to looking over the edge of the cliff although he had believed he was looking at a field. 'It is odd that I walked over a "ghostly path" and "ghostly field" and these did not disappear, but the wall and field at the edge of the cliff did. The danger must have been so apparent to my sub-conscious mind that it broke the spell.'

An important point was the discovery, on the Friday, of a fragment of wall on the headland. Some three weeks later a cliff fall occurred, taking with it the wall.

Mr Spence's statement given above was analysed by a correspondent, Mr J. T. Evans, in the December 1947 issue of the *Journal*, and from this it is clear where the experience took place, Crabrock Point at Man Sands, near Brixham. Mr Evans pointed out that the cave, passing underneath Crabrock Point, must be known to many people. The north-west opening, a small one in a little inlet at the southern end of Man Sands, was above the high-water mark but the floor of the south-east opening was under water even at low spring tides. In the cliff face above the north-west opening, the one referred to in the statement, there was a shatter-zone of loose material from which it was evident that falls of shale were not uncommon; loose shale lies in a large heap on the floor of this entrance to the cave and largely obscures it. Mr Spence's suggestion that there had been a landslip between the Tuesday and the Thursday visits was quite likely and this was a normal occurrence.

Mr Spence said that he had clambered up a little cliff path on the Tuesday but could not find it on the Thursday when he looked for it from above. There were two rough paths up the cliff at the southern end of Man Sands. One of them was not very obvious and having 'clambered up' it on Tuesday Mr Spence might well have had difficulty in finding it again when he approached it from above on Thursday.

As regards the field, Mr Spence said that in the field between the cove and the wall he found more bracken on Tuesday and Thursday than he did on Wednesday. Mr Evans pointed out that on Tuesday and Thursday the route taken was not far from the cliff edge and lay between bracken and brambles. On Wednesday the route was inland and lay over grass. The 1/2,500 Ordnance map showed that the cliff-side route may well have had more bracken and brambles than the inland route and there seemed nothing abnormal about the varied vegetation. What would seem abnormal was the presence of high bracken at all in March.

The statement said that a lone tree and gate were visible from the wall on the Wednesday but on the Tuesday merely a mass of stunted trees could be seen at first and the lone tree and gate appeared as Mr Spence walked on. According to Mr Evans, the

117

ground rose steeply from Man Sands to the old wall and thence to the triangulation point, indicated as a small triangle on the Ordnance map, on the shoulder of the hill, and thereafter it rose more gently to the gate, which was not visible from the old wall; the shoulder of the hill intervened. On walking southward from the wall towards the gate the first objects to appear were several stunted wind-driven trees on and below the edge of the cliff. Then the gate became apparent. On walking south-westward from the wall, however, the gate was clearly seen, owing to undulations in the surface of the ground, before the stunted trees came into view. 'Considering that the land surface here undulates steeply in two directions so that it is confusing and most difficult to keep accurate account of movements or direction and considering that the statement was written eighteen months after the event, the account of the relative visibility of the gate and the stunted trees is surprisingly accurate and it discloses nothing abnormal.' Mr Evans considered that on one point alone Mr Spence's memory appeared to be at fault. The statement that the gate was visible from the place where the fall nearly took place was not correct; the shoulder of the hill intervenes.

Mr Spence's statement said that on the Tuesday and Thursday the wall seemed less ivy-covered but longer than it did on Wednesday. Mr Evans considered that the apparent change and condition and length of the wall might possibly have been due to the following two features: (1) part of the wall was ivy-covered, particularly near the point where the fall nearly took place, and part was free from ivy; (2) the edge of the cliff was not well defined but grew progressively steeper and the vegetation made it difficult to see where the steep part of the cliff began and where the wall ended. On the Thursday Mr Spence thought the wall extended for some way over grass and brambles and bracken to the verge of the cliff, but on taking a few paces forward he felt giddy and nearly fell over the edge. The dense vegetation made it easy to approach the edge of the cliff near the wall without realizing the danger of falling until one was actually on a steep incline and this may be what actually happened in 1938.

As regards the tide, the statement said that on the Tuesday the tide was out and Mr Spence was able to enter the cave, but on Wednesday and Thursday at about the same time as on Tuesday the tide was in and the cave inlet was under water. Mr Evans pointed out that the approach to the inlet in which the cave was situated was cut off at high tide. On the Tuesday, high tide was recorded at 9.34 a.m. and it was assumed that Mr Spence arrived at the beach some time later in the morning when the tide had fallen some distance. He was able to enter the cave inlet. On the Wednesday, when he arrived at about the same time, the tide was higher, since it gained thirty or forty minutes each day, and the approach to the inlet was cut off. On the Thursday, the tide was higher still and Mr Spence had to wait for it to fall before being able to reach the cave inlet.

These conditions were what would normally be expected and no explanation would be necessary were it not that the tide was stated to have been 'right out' on Tuesday and 'right up' at about the same time on Wednesday and Thursday.

Two points should be noted, Mr Evans said: (1) the sandy part of the beach at Man Sands was flat, and thirty or forty minutes made a considerable difference to the appearance of the beach; moreover, the sand elsewhere was broader and higher than in the immediate neighbourhood of the cave inlet and a large expanse of sand was exposed not far away at the time when the tide looked lower elsewhere than at the cave inlet; and (2) the tide on the Wednesday and Thursday was described variously as being 'right up', 'fairly full' and 'practically full' so that it seems possible that the tidal conditions and the times of arrival were not observed with much precision.

The hallucinatory explanation requires either that Mr Spence really walked across the beach at high tide on Tuesday under the impression that it was low tide, without even getting his clothes wet, or else that the whole Tuesday visit was an hallucination. Both these explanations seem more difficult to accept than the one suggested above, namely, that his three visits were made round about that state of the tide at which the approach to the cave inlet became uncovered.

At the end of his discussion on all the features of Mr Spence's experience, Mr Evans's conclusion was that 'the cumulative effect of these apparently abnormal features must have been impressive to the observer but it is difficult to say, on the information available, that the experiences were so unusual as to preclude the possibility of normal explanations'.

The editor of the *Journal* commented:

This case is not evidential. We have to take the narrator's word for what happened, for the experience was a solitary one and corroboration is impossible. There was a lapse of some eighteen months before the account was written. However, granting the integrity of the witness, it is very difficult to attribute the supposed experience to a trick of memory or other form of self-deception. There is the photograph mentioned in the account, and other photographs of the old wall, which Mr Spence has sent to the Society. There is the startling fact that at one stage he attempted to step into thin air. There is considerable psychological interest in a hallucination so strong that it caused the percipient to step off a cliff under impression that he was walking along a path, while at the same time he felt giddy as if standing on a great height. The behaviour of the tide is most curious. While under the influence of the hallucination, it seemed to Mr Spence that the tide was far out and that he was crossing the beach, whereas in fact the tide was in and this would be impossible.

Mr Spence said he checked the state of the tides at once. He also mentioned the incident to his uncle, with whom he was staying at the time. In a note to the research officer dated 3 June 1947 Mr Spence's uncle said that he remembered that his nephew did mention something of his strange experience at Man Sands, but it was so long ago that he really could not remember any details. All he could say was that he was 'somewhat amazed' at the time.

Commenting on the case in his *Ghosts of the Trianon* Dr Coleman said that it presented several interesting parallels with *An Adventure*: it was not reported for some months and not investigated for some years, and the visionary scene was encountered more than once. Also in both cases the percipient experienced a sense of depression throughout the hallucinatory episodes. Since Mr Spence was unaccompanied on each occasion of his visits to Man Sands, there was of course no question of corroboration, but even accepting Mr Spence's account at face value, it obviously contains nothing beyond the scope of rational inference.

Summing up, Dr Coleman concludes that 'Altogether there seems little justification for regarding Mr Spence's experiences as founded on anything other that a few misperceptions'.

When we analyse this case we find that there is no single item of the scenery reported by Mr Spence that could be attributed to the past but was not there in 1938. There were sections of old wall and new wall, stunted trees and undergrowth of various kinds. If this was all there was to the experiences on the three days of Mr Spence's visits, retrocognition could be ruled out. Mr Spence does not seem to have taken account of the fact that there were two cliff paths when he compiled his account, although they are shown on the map which accompanied his statement, and he was obviously wrong about the state of the tide. If, when the tide is up, you attempt to walk across what seems to you to be a stretch of exposed beach you will take only a step or two before you realize you are getting very wet indeed.

This said, we should now turn our attention to Mr Spence's experience on the cliff edge when he nearly fell, possibly to his death, and his state of mind during the three visits. Mr Spence attributed his giddiness to looking over the edge of the cliff although he thought he was looking at a field and commented: 'it is odd that I walked over a "ghostly path" and "ghostly field" and these did not disappear, but the wall and field at the edge of the cliff did'. In short, Mr Spence thought he was continuing his walk to a cliff edge he saw in front of him without realizing that his had been hallucinated and that the actual cliff edge was at his feet. Fortunately, because of his giddiness, he stopped and, pulling his camera from his pocket, took a photograph which, when developed and reproduced in the SPR *Journal*, showed a view from the cliff edge on to rocks below. On the day following his near fall Mr Spence discovered a fragment of wall nearby, but some three weeks later a cliff fall occurred, taking with it the wall.

This fact, I believe, offers a clue to what Mr Spence experienced. In his hallucinatory experience he 'saw' fields and wall which had once existed but which had disappeared during cliff falls.

Mr Spence set out in detail his states of mind during his experiences and these are so similar to those in the Kersey case that they indicate to me that Mr Spence did indeed have a retrocognitive experience. In both cases there was the sensation of being watched, feelings of depression and fear, the cessation of birdsong or bird calls (as a rule coastal areas in England are alive with the screams of seagulls), and an unnatural silence (Mr Spence described this as 'awful'). On his first visit this silence lasted for half an hour ('for the first time since I had entered the cove about half an hour earlier, I heard a definitely real sound: a seagull flew over my head screaming'). There are indications in both cases of a change in seasons in the hallucinated landscape: there was a springlike freshness and greenness in the Kersey Mr Laing saw, although the month was October, and Mr Spence, walking on the cliffs, was 'surprised to find on looking back that the grass seemed greener and fresher and the bracken less than when I had passed through it'.

There was, however, one feature of Mr Spence's experiences which was most distinctive and which I have not come across elsewhere: 'the impression that something was straining at a leash so that one could almost hear the noise that something made, trying to break the bonds'. This was on the Tuesday. Mr Spence had the same feeling on the Thursday but on a much larger scale. He likened this impression to that of 'a cart-horse straining at a wagon-load of bricks which it could not possibly drag'.

Mr Laing and his companions saw no one in the Kersey they visited in 1957. On his first visit to the cove Mr Spence 'felt even more depressed and lonely than before'. He does not mention seeing anybody on his later visits to the cliffs, although others may have been there. If so, they were excluded from the scenery of the present day.

Mr Spence sent the account of his experiences to the society after he had read *An Adventure* because he detected some similarities between what had occurred to him in Devonshire and the experiences of Miss Moberly and Miss Jourdain in Versailles. A common feature of both was the feeling of depression. Another was the fact that the state of what may be termed trance was variable. Mr Spence said that 'if I got some glimpse of this corner of the world as it was, possibly centuries ago, I must have been under that spell only for certain definite periods', and it is clear to anyone who reads *An Adventure* carefully that the fact that the two ladies did not always see the same features of the park or the same figures together indicates that they were in differing states of consciousness.

As the editor of the *Journal* observed in publishing this case, 'There is considerable psychological interest in a hallucination so strong that it caused the percipient to step off a cliff under the impression that he was walking along a path, while at the same time he felt giddy as if standing on a great height'. This remark goes to the heart of the matter. Although we may have reservations about some parts of Mr Spence's narrative, and how they may be interpreted, there can be little doubt about the reality of the episode on the cliffs when the path he thought he was treading proved not to be there. Even if the whole account is disputed, it is surely very odd that the states of mind Mr Spence described should tally so closely with those of others who have recounted similar retrocognitive experiences.

Chapter 11

Seeking an Answer

When we look back on the cases I have presented we cannot escape the feeling that we have been lunged into a very strange world, one that many of us have never encountered, but this is not a sufficient reason for dismissing the accounts of those who have had the experiences described. The 'things like that don't happen' argument is not relevant because some leading physicists have agreed that backward causation can be accepted. This, in turn, means that we have to set aside the argument that time 'flows'. In *The Emperor's New Mind* Roger Penrose suggests that we may actually be going badly wrong if we apply the usual physical rules for *time* when we consider consciousness:

> There is, indeed, something very odd about the way that time actually enters into our conscious perceptions in any case, and I think that it is possible that a very different conception may be required when we try to place conscious perceptions into a conventionally time-ordered framework. Consciousness is, after all, the one phenomenon that we know of, according to which time needs to 'flow' at all! The way in which time is treated in modern physics is not essentially different from the way in which *space* is treated and the 'time' of physical descriptions does not really 'flow' at all; we just have a static-looking fixed 'space-time' in which the events of our universe are laid out! My guess is that there is something illusory here too, and the time of our perceptions does not 'really' flow in quite the linear forward-moving way that we perceive it to flow (whatever that might mean!). The temporal ordering that we 'appear' to perceive is, I am claiming, something that we impose upon our perceptions in order to make sense of them in relation to the uniform forward time-progression of an external physical reality.

Once we have grasped that time does not flow in the way we had been accustomed to think it did, the realization that retrocognitive experiences can occur should not surprise us.

However, the immediate reaction of readers will be that they are only too well aware of the passage of time, from morning to evening, and from childhood to old age, and how can we explain that away?

Professor J. R. Smythies, a consultant neuropsychiatrist, discusses this problem in a review of Penrose's book in the *Journal* of the SPR. Here he asks:

> what then is the distortion of experience engineered by the 'illusion' of the passage of time? It could only be that time does not flow, has stopped or never got going. But we do not live in the world of the Mad Hatter's tea party where it is always teatime. So what generates this illusion? The *sense* of the rate of passage of time can, of course, be enormously slowed down or speeded up by drugs. But even here time never stops completely. A world in which time does not flow is more than a world in which all movements stop and all clocks remain pointing to four o'clock. We can imagine living in such a paralysed world in which no movement ever occurs. But even in such a world our conscious sense of time passing would still exist. In order to know that the clock had stopped we would have to look at it several times. But would consciousness itself continue? The stoping of time would halt all neuronal processes in the brain. Irreversible death would not occur since no degenerative processes would take place either, and if time started up again, the brain would simply go on as before. But it seems difficult to imagine how consciousness, as we know it, could continue without any brain processes going on at all. So the real state of which Penrose's 'illusion' is a distortion would appear to be the complete obliteration of consciousness in any form that we know it. In which case it seems quite unallowable to call a distortion of nothing an illusion. But perhaps Penrose meant to say that our subjective sense of the passage of time is an hallucination, which, by definition, does not have any reality behind it. But does it make sense to call something that everyone experiences every day of their lives 'hallucinatory'? If one has ordinary hallucinations it is always possible to imagine what things would

be like not to have hallucinations. Can we imagine what it would be like to exist without the hallucination that time is passing? Again, however, we can only equate a state of consciousness in which we had no sense of the flow of time, with the complete abolition of consciousness itself.

Professor Smythies concludes that 'The passage of time is as real as any phenomenon could be. It can be accounted for perfectly easily by a dualist theory of mind.'

The second point we should grasp is that experiences involving retrocognition occur in certain states of mind that, so far as we know, cannot be anticipated or induced. As John Beloff points out in *The Relentless Question*, 'Psi phenomena are problematic because they involve events in the real world and thus become candidates for a physical explanation yet at the same time they are critically bound up with certain states of mind. Thus they cross the dividing line between objectivity and subjectivity which normal phenomena do not.'

Here we are facing a real mystery. Reviewing Colin McGinn's book *The Problem of Consciousness* in *The London Review of Books*, Professor Jerry Fodor, of Rutgers University, stated that 'If, as McGinn supposes, the problem about consciousness really isn't just a muddle, then there is something going on that we deeply do not understand, something that our best science gives no hint of accommodating.'

Another real mystery we must face is how we are to explain those cases in which people see buildings, presumably of the past, that never existed. We may attempt an answer under what we may call the 'imprint' theory, as set out by the late Professor H. H. Price, who held the chair of Wykeham Professor of Logic at Oxford University, in his presidential address to the SPR on 'Haunting and the "psychic ether" hypothesis'. It concerns *mental images*, and Price advances the idea that once an image has come into being, it has the tendency to *persist* in being, and that it is not dependent upon the mind for its continuance. Price went on to say that images not only were persistent entities, but were endowed with causal properties. 'If you prefer to put it so, we will say that they are "dynamic" rather than "static" entities, endowed with a kind of "force" of their own.'

Psychic ether, Price suggested, consists of traces which were not material in the ordinary sense, but somehow interpenetrated the walls or the furniture: 'something which was like matter in being extended, and yet like mind in that it retained in itself the residue of past experiences'.

Professor Price admitted that the theory of haunting he advanced was 'much too narrow' in that he had spoken as if images were the only sort of psychical contents, which was far from true. Again, the theory had in any case been restricted to one special type of haunting, the type in which there were no physical effects: it could only be extended to cover other types by introducing additional assumptions, which might have to be 'very outrageous'.

If we accept Professor Price's view of the persistence of images which assume a life of their own we have, I feel, a clue to a possible answer to the puzzle posed by the perception of the spectral houses described in Chapter 6. Different people at different places saw houses which they were unable to find again, despite a diligent search, and which, later inquiry proved, had never stood on the spot where they were seen.

Take, for instance, the Georgian house behind a high wall at Bradfield St George seen by Miss Wynne and her pupil Miss Allington during a walk in October 1926 but which they were unable to find during later visits to the area. Let us suppose that someone had once planned such a house on the site and visualized what it would look like behind a wall of greenish-yellow brick. Events, however, intervened, or possibly the man who planned the house suffered a financial loss, and the house was never built. With Price's theory in mind, is it not possible that the two young women, perhaps standing where the prospective builder had once stood, 'picked up' his image of the house?

Likewise, the house seen in a field in another part of the village by Mr Robert Palfrey in 1860, by his great-grandson around 1908 and by other villagers could have been the image of a house once planned for the site but never built.

The other house mentioned in this chapter, seen by Miss Grace MacMahon and her brother during a walk in a wood in Essex, was an imposing Georgian one and hurrying down the drive from it was a young girl dressed in contemporary clothes and accompanied by an Alsatian dog. Inquiries revealed that a house had never stood on that site. However, could someone have planned a house there and stood where Miss MacMahon and her brother did, visualizing how his daughter and the family dog would fit into the scene?

This sounds very far-fetched, and highly speculative, but it is in accord with Professor Price's theory of how images can persist and take on a life of their own. I can think of no other theory that can explain the phenomena involving spectral houses described in Chapter 6. However, we must bear in mind that possibly the cases I have quoted were simply hallucinations of a rather complex kind, although it is surely rather strange that the experiences of various people in Bradfield St George all took the same form, that of seeing houses in places where house had never been built.

It is important to understand that retrocognition is, as a rule, linked to what is experienced at a certain spot. But why, the reader may ask, should this be so? F. W. H. Myers, one of the pioneers of psychical research (see the Appendix) addressed this problem when he advanced the concept of what he called a 'phantasmogenetic centre'; he described this as 'a point in space so modified by the presence of a spirit that it becomes perceptible to persons near it. The concept of a *psychical excursion* or *invasion* implies that some movement bearing some relation to space as we know it is accomplished; that the invading spirit modifies a certain portion of space, not materially or optically, but in such a manner that specially susceptible persons may perceive it.' I feel that these days we may set aside Myers's belief that an invading spirit was the cause of the modification of space, or what we would today call space-time, but the concept is deeply interesting. Discussing the theory in this book *Mediumship and Survival* (1982) Alan Gauld concedes that perhaps a scene is 'somehow imprinted or recorded on the physical locality in which it happened, perhaps there is a recurring kink or loop in space-time at that point . . . the percipients "tune-in" or slip out of present time for a moment'. I feel I should point out that in some of the experiences I have related here people 'tuned-in' or 'slipped out' of the present time not for a moment but for as long as half an hour, as happened in the Versailles or Kersey cases, and this could have been prolonged if the people concerned had stayed longer on the scene. What was involved in the cases I have quoted was a long period of dislocation of space-time.

There is a connection, I feel, between cases of haunting and retrocognition because both involve the reaction of people to places. Certain houses or spots are places to which some people, according to their sensitivity or personality structure, react strongly. In scientific terms this may be regarded as the 'feedback' of the place to one of the persons there. This 'feedback' can take various forms, from a feeling of happiness to acute depression. I have quoted a number of cases in which a feeling of depression accompanied a retrocognitive experience. If this concept is thought fanciful, I could cite a number of cases in which people visiting a house with a view to purchasing it did not do so because they disliked the atmosphere of the place.

In his masterly *Human Personality and its Survival of Bodily Death* (1903) Myers said:

> I think that the curious question as to the influence of certain *houses* in generating apparitions may be included under the broader heading of Retrocognition. That is to say, we are not here dealing with a special condition of certain houses, but with a branch of the wide problem as to the nature of phenomena to *time*. Manifestations which occur in haunted houses depend, let us say, on something which has taken place a long time ago. In what way do they depend on that past event? Are they a sequel or only a residue? Is there a fresh operation going on, or only fresh perception of something already accomplished? Or can we in such a case draw any real distinction between a continued action and a continued perception of a past action? The closest parallel, as it seems to me, although not at first sight an obvious one, lies between these phenomena of haunting, these persistent sights and sounds, and certain phenomena of crystal vision and of automatic script, which also seem to depend somehow upon long-past events, – to be the sequel of their residue.
>
> (1903: Vol 2, p.76)

Myers and other writers have pointed out that psychometry, a practice in which sensitives hold an object in their hands and obtain impressions of a paranormal nature about the object or its past owners, often provides examples of apparent retrocognition.

It is now time to finish our study of retrocognition. I have drawn attention to the fact that the subject does not conflict with the findings of modern physics about backward causation and that in some of the cases given here, notably in Part One, information which could be verified was provided. I have left to the last what is probably the most convincing evidence for the reality of the phenomena described here – they form a natural group. That Myers realized this is indicated in a paper he published in the *Proceedings* of the SPR more than a century ago in which he said:

> retrocognition and precognition – supernormal knowledge of Past and Future – cannot be set aside as isolated problems; – as fortresses which we may leave behind us unattacked as we advance over our newly conquered realm. On the contrary, our work tends to become more and more emphatically an *exploration of faculty*; – not merely a collection of evidence of particular occurrences, but a following out of every clue which may lead to knowledge of what is actually going on beneath the threshold while certain resulting phenomena are showing above it. We must search for the *natural groups* into which our cases fall; contenting ourselves no longer with the first obvious line of classification.
>
> (1895: 336)

Just as there are patterns in illness that are clear to the physician as indications of a particular malady, so patterns may be discerned in certain cases which suggest that they belong to examples of retrocognition. In nearly all such cases it is clear that the subjects are hallucinated, a state accompanied by feelings of depression, uneasiness, a sense of danger and, in certain instances, particularly in Chapters 1(Kersey) and 4 (Versailles), not only by the substitution of the scenery of the present for that of the past but also the elimination of people of the present day. What I found particularly interesting in the accounts was the description of the rather eerie sense of silence that accompanied some of the experiences – 'a silence out of this world' in Kersey, according to Mr Laing, and, in Versailles, 'the extreme silence and stillness of the place', which struck Miss Moberly and Miss Jourdain. During the visit of Mr Wilkinson and his family to the Grand Trianon in 1949, when they saw the apparition of a woman in a crinoline dress, he noted the 'noticeable quiet and stillness about the place'. When young John Watson had his vision of a vanished street in Nottingham in 1961 'the street was surprisingly quiet for somewhere near a city centre'. In the Preface I have quoted Miss Jourdain's words: her feeling that she was 'being taken up into another condition of things quite as real as the former' when the shrill voices of the quarrelling women died away during the change in the landscape.

This could be expressed as a feeling that she was moving into another dimension.

The examples I have quoted come from real life and contain so many elements in common that they form a pattern that should not be ignored. However, they surely form only a small fraction of those that have occurred and have never been reported. How many experiences similar to those of the three youths in Kersey in 1957, which set me thinking along the lines that have resulted in the appearance of this book, the first to be devoted solely to retrocogniton, have yet to come to light? As Dr Gauld said in his Introduction, 'Our prime need is for more data.' If you know of examples of retrocognition and haunting, please write to me at the Society for Psychical Research, 49 Marloes Road, Kensington, London W8 6LA. Names and addresses will not be revealed without the permission of the correspondent.

Appendix

The word 'retrocognition' was first used by F. W. H. Myers in 1892 in the *Proceedings* of the SPR (Vol 8). He defined it in his last work, *Human Personality*, as 'knowledge of the past, supernormally acquired'. In a passage in the same work he declared that 'supernormal retrocognition depends, it appears, on the perception by us of knowledge contained in other minds, embodied or disembodied, and possibly on the absorption by us of knowledge afloat, so to say, in the Universe – which may be grasped by our spirit's outreaching, or which may fall on us like dew'.

In an important paper in SPR *Proceedings* (Vol 11) in 1895, Myers said that we have to consider whether any of the phenomena of retrocognition which lie before us are explicable as extensions of organic memory – as evocations into daylight consciousness of imprints made in this life, or in ancestral lives, upon our physical being:

> So much of intellectual predisposition is hereditary that it would be rash to fix *a priori* any point where a memory was too definite to be capable of transmission. It is a question of evidence; but I may say at once that for an ancestral memory as definite as would here be needed there seems to me to be at present no adequate evidence, and that the hypothesis is worth mentioning mainly because any other explanation of some of these facts or pictures from a remote past . . . seems at first to be still more incredible.
>
> (1895: 350)

Myers regarded the memories of departed spirits as 'constituting a real and most important source of retrocognition', but pointed out that even when we are dealing with true retrocognition involving scenes or histories in which men long departed have played their part we must not assume that such knowledge must needs have come to us through the agency of some definite and assignable discarnate mind. For aught we know the scene may come to us without any such intervention. 'Its permanence in the Universe cannot depend upon its relation to any finite mind. If one image persists, then all images; for the omnipresent mind includes them all . . . . Nothing for that intelligence is drowned in the deeps of an infinite Past.'

A later scholar, W. H. W. Sabine, seems to have been thinking along the same lines when he said in an important paper, 'Is there a case for retrocognition?', in the *Journal* of the American SPR for April 1950 – one of the few to be devoted to this subject – that though the word 'retrocognition' was not applicable to the individual memory of the past, it would be possible to apply it to individual access to a universal memory, one in which are stored all the mental impressions of all the minds of all time. 'Such a collective memory would amount to the permanent existence of all past events that had been known to any mind, and access to such a memory would be as effective retrocognition as perception of the event itself.'

Mr Sabine strikes a controversial note when he says that we are not justified in classifying as retrocognitive any cases of the possession or acquisition of normally inexplicable knowledge of the past so long as any person is living who had the knowledge by normal means. 'Nor can we regard as conclusive any cases of apparent retrocognition when the information concerned exists in books, manuscripts, hidden articles, buried foundations of buildings, and so on. Such instances are attributable to forms or aspects of extra-normal cognition which have been accepted as conclusively proven by many qualified investigators.'

He is here invoking the super-ESP hypothesis that since there are no known limits to the scope of *psi*, extra-sensory perception of the past by the living could explain acquisition of knowledge covering as wide a field as he sets out above. A number of 'qualified investigators' would disagree with him. For instance, discussing survival in this book *Mediumship and Survival*, Alan Gauld says:

Certain mediumistic communications and certain ostensibly reincarnated personalities display so many correct and detailed apparent memories of a previous existence on earth that ESP by medium or reincarnated subject scarcely seems a possible explanation, unless, indeed, we are prepared to postulate ESP of an extent and complexity for which we have no independent support . . . . The super-ESP hypothesis suffers from a large credibility gap.

(1982: 188)

Another doubter is Dr Karlis Osis, the recently retired director of research at the American SPR. Discussing apparitions in that society's *Newsletter* for summer 1990 he said:

the exact nature of stimuli in collective cases in still unknown, but apparitions that are collectively seen do suggest a disembodied agency. Numerous attempts have been made to explain them, such as the super-ESP hypothesis. However, these explanations have been severely criticized . . . because ESP of the magnitude and reliability needed to account for the observed phenomena have not been found.

I feel that Dr Osis's remarks about attempts to explain away cases of the collective perception of apparitions by recourse to the super-ESP hypothesis could equally well apply to attempts to explain away examples of apparent retrocognition.

Mr Sabine states that 'It is evident that the difficulty which confronts us in the case of apparent retrocognition is similar to and even greater than that presented by apparent spirit communications. Precisely what information of the past could we accept as satisfactory?'

This question deserves a careful answer. There will always be doubt, I feel, about experiences involving the perception of people of a past age because questions could arise about the identity of the persons involved. For instance, Miss Moberly and Miss Jourdain assumed that the 'sketching lady' they saw during their visit to the grounds of the Petit Trianon in 1901 was the apparition of Marie Antoinette as she was in 1789, but in this they were almost certainly wrong for reasons I have already explained in the chapter devoted to that case. It is much safer to rely on geographical features as a guide to a certain period. Later research than that undertaken by Miss Moberly and Miss Jourdain indicates that what they 'saw' was the park of the Petit Trianon, and the building itself, as in 1770–71, a date that never occurred to the ladies.

Likewise, the three youths who entered Kersey in 1957 saw a butcher's shop where one had once stood, although there was no indication of this at the time of their visit. Mr Watson (Chapter 2) described correctly a street he 'saw' in Nottingham in 1961 as it was before it was destroyed in 1956, and Mrs McAvoy (Chapter 3) 'saw' in a little village in the Highlands a house that had stood on a certain site nearly two hundred years earlier, although there was no indication, not even a ruin, to lead her to think that what she saw had some basis in reality.

I feel that the information of the past provided by the cases I have quoted can be regarded as satisfactory.

Myers's most important paper on retrocognition was written more than a century ago and Mr Sabine's, from which I have just quoted, more than forty years ago. Since then the subject has been neglected in the literature of psychical research, which is surely strange in view of the insights provided by physicists as the result of their researches.

Selected Bibliography

Amadou, R., Moberly, C. A. E. and Jourdain, E. F., *Les Fantômes de Trianon*, Paris: Editions du Rocher, 1976.

Beloff, J., *The Relentless Question: Reflections on the Paranormal*, Jefferson, NC and London: McFarland, 1990.

Bennett, Sir Ernest, *Apparitions and Haunted Houses*, London: Faber, 1939.

Brown, R. L., *A Casebook of Military Mystery*, Cambridge: Patrick Stephen, 1974; this book contains a number of accounts of battles fought by phantom armies.

Coleman, M. H., *The Ghosts of the Trianon*, Wellingborough, Northants: Aquarian, 1988.

Davies, P., *God and the New Physics*, London: Dent, 1983; Harmondsworth: Penguin edition, 1984.

Evans, J., Preface to the 5th edition of C. A. E. Moberly and E. F. Jourdain, *An Adventure*, London: Faber, 1955.

Forman, J., *The Mask of Time*, London: Macdonald & Jane's, 1978.

Gauld, A., *Mediumship and Survival*, London: Heinemann, 1982.

Gibbons, O. A. and Gibbons, M. E., *The Trianon Adventure: a Symposium*, London: Museum Press, 1958.

Hastings, R. J., 'An examination of the Dieppe Raid case', *Journal of the Society for Psychical Research*, 55 (1969): 66–175.

Hawking, S. W., *A Brief History of Time*, London: Bantam Press, 1988.

Iremonger, L., *The Ghosts of Versailles: a Critical Study*, London: Faber, 1957.

Jaffé, A., *Apparitions and Precognition: a Study from the Point of View of C. G. Jung's Analytical Psychology*, New York: University Books, 1963.

Lambert, G. W., 'Antoine Richard's garden: a postscript to *An Adventure*', *Journal of the Society for Psychical Research*, 37 (1953): 117–54.

—— 'Antoine Richard's garden: a postscript to *An Adventure*' (continued), *Journal of the Society for Psychical Research*, 37 (1954): 266–79.

—— 'Antoine Richard's garden: a supplementary note', *Journal of the Society for Psychical Research*, 38 (1955): 12–18.

—— 'Additional investigations', in O. A. Gibbons and M. E. Gibbons, *The Trianon Adventure: a Symposium*, London: Museum Press, 1958.

—— 'Richard's garden revisited', *Journal of the Society for Psychical Research*, 41 (1962): 279–92.

—— 'Phantom scenery', *Journal of the Society for Psychical Research*, 42, 715 (March 1963): 1–6.

—— 'Phantom scenery: chapter two', *Journal of the Society for Psychical Research*, 42, 721 (September 1964): 348–52.

Lambert, G. W. and Gay, K. 'The Dieppe Raid case', *Journal of the Society for Psychical Research*, 670 (May–June 1952): 607–18.

McHarg, J., 'A vision of the aftermath of the battle of Nechtanesmere, AD 685', *Journal of the Society for Psychical Research*, 49, 778 (December 1978): 938–48.

MacKenzie, A., *The Unexplained*, London: Arthur Barker, 1966.

—— *Hauntings and Apparitions*, London: Heinemann, 1982.

Moberly, C. A. E. and Jourdain, E. F., *An Adventure*, London: Macmillan, 1911; 4th edition, London: Faber, 1931; 5th edition, London: Faber, 1955.

Myers, F. W. H., 'The relation of supernormal phenomena to time-retrocognition', *Proceedings of the Society for Psychical Research*, 29, 11 (December 1895).

—— *Human Personality and its Survival of Bodily Death*, London: Longman, 1903.

Olivier, Edith, Introduction to the 4th edition of C. A. E. Moberly and E. F. Jourdain, *An Adventure*, London: Faber, 1931.

Osis, K., 'Title at proof', newsletter of the American Society for Psychical Research' (summer 1990).

Penrose, R., *The Emperor's New Mind*, New York: Oxford University Press, 1989; London: Vintage edition, 1990.

Price, H. H., 'Haunting and the "psychic ether" hypothesis', *Proceedings of the Society for Psychical Research*, 45 (1938–9): 307–41.

Sabine, W. H. W., 'Is there a case for retrocognition?', *Journal of*

the American Society for Psychical Research, 44, 2 (April 1950)
44–64.

Schmidt, H., 'PK effect on three recorded targets', *Journal of the Society for Psychical Research*, 70 (1976): 267–93.

Smythies, J. R., 'Mind, brain, space, time: an essay review of Roger Penrose's *The Emperor's New Mind*', *Journal of the Society for Psychical Research*, 36, 820 (July 1990) 229–234.

Sturge-Whiting, J., *The Mystery of Versailles*, London: Occult Book Society, 1937.

Wainwright, F. T., 'Nechtanesmere', *Antiquity*, 22 (1948): 82–97.

Yarwood, D., *The English Home*, London: Batsford, 1979.

Index